|||| Manuel ||||

MANUEL

by Christopher Jackson

NEW YORK · ALFRED · A · KNOPF · 1964

L. C. catalog card number: 64–12314

THIS IS A BORZOI BOOK,
PUBLISHED BY ALFRED A. KNOPF, INC.

FIRST EDITION

FOR
Francisco
&
Ramón
Layera
Jiménez

WITH AFFECTION

Contents IIII

IIII Manuel IIII

Prologue IIII

I

IIII   This book arose out of a chance invitation from a student. While we were talking together at my home one day in June 1962, he mentioned that his father had been governor of the city prison and that his elder brother, who had followed in his father's footsteps, was now an officer there. He then invited me to look it over with him. To be frank, I was embarrassed by an invitation which I was both eager and reluctant to accept. At different times in my life—in India during the war, in South Africa, in Italy—I had seen poverty and human helplessness and degradation. But since this experience had come my way as a by-product of my day-to-day work, while I was serving in Intelligence or teaching philosophy to African students or studying Italian art, I felt a tyro, and shrank from encountering human misery face to face. So I evaded the invitation with cagey thanks, and turned the talk to other matters.

Two months later, however, I took him up on it. Fear and shame had given place to a more overpowering emotion. I wanted to meet a murderer. He was a young man of seventeen who had confessed to a crime that had provoked a good deal of public argument. This was partly due to the character and social status of the victim and partly to its thriller interest, but mainly to its circumstances. An elderly lawyer, prominent in Valparaíso society, had been battered to death in his office by a young man he had apparently invited in. The

4

murderer had ransacked the room but taken almost nothing. In the few days that elapsed before his capture he had behaved with a mixture of coolness, daring, and folly so striking as to suggest a more subtle interpretation of his motives than the obvious one of robbery. Moreover, his subsequent "confession," which destroyed the reputation of the dead man and created considerable sympathy for the boy, was yet very odd and baffling.

Good-looking, vain, and highly talkative, this self-confessed young murderer was mild-mannered, soft-spoken, and considerably better educated than most boys of his class. In many ways he was a typical poor boy of the streets: without a settled home life, lacking skills, and chronically unemployed, he lived fecklessly from hand to mouth on odd jobs, drifting easily and pointlessly into crime. He was also a Teddy boy who sported, when he could afford it, the flashy uniform *de rigueur* at that time in his group. He had a record of petty crime behind him; on his own confession, he had been an armed robber, forger, and male prostitute, and had no objection to blackmail. He was now charged with murder. By any rational standard, his crime seemed entirely senseless and the record of his behavior, as he presented it, quite inexplicable. I wanted to make sense of both of them. Or, to speak more accurately, I wanted to make sense of him: to see his life as he himself saw it, to obtain some understanding of his own estimate of his acts.

I had no special equipment for this self-imposed task.

True, I was born in Valparaíso, of an English family which for at least three generations had lived in South America. For the past seven years I had been working in Valparaíso as professor of English literature in the national university, and had many Chilean friends and relations. But my background and qualifications—such as they were—seemed a mixed blessing. A traditional English education in the ancient classics, followed by an Oxford degree in philosophy; a professional life spent in research or teaching in English-speaking universities; a literary cast of mind; a donnish manner and a modest Chair might mark their possessor as a run of the mill academic or an English gentleman, but they could hardly be said to furnish a passport to the confidence of a young Chilean criminal, much less a key to the freedom of the city of which he alone was master. A little over forty, an alien, and a don: I entered his world as a stranger, unaccredited. I had everything to learn.

When I started, I thought I would find a "little boy lost"; I envisaged him encased within a tight, self-enclosed social cocoon, with its own standards and system of values, supported by a clear code, fighting an unending battle against Them, that hostile nation. I suspected that the circumstances of his life had pushed him into crime, that his thefts were products as much of accident as of design, and that the murder he had committed had its roots in fright, disgust, despair. His family, friends, and fellow prisoners would present me, I imagined, if I met them, with a picture markedly

6

different in tone and feeling from that provided by the law, the police, the press. I guessed that his story, if he cared to tell it, would throw far more light on the conditions of the poor in Chile than on the factors commonly assumed to be responsible for crime.

In some, rather limited ways I was right in my assumptions; but mainly I was wrong. Even when a general idea was correct in principle, its relevance proved quite different from what I had anticipated. I learned most when I was unlearning what I had taken for granted. Manuel Garcés, the murderer, *was* a "little boy lost"; but this image proved altogether misleading. He inspired great compassion; there was never any doubt of the depth of his need—for love, for attention, for genuine human concern. His case moved two lawyers to offer him their services for a nominal fee; it led me in search of him myself. Yet he was peculiarly unlikable. He was young, well-built, quite intelligent; he told his story very well. One would have expected closer acquaintance to provoke almost instinctively sympathetic feeling. It did not. He was entirely self-absorbed and self-centered. In the seven months I knew him, I can think of only one friendly question he ever asked concerning the life of anyone other than himself, and I should be hard put to name half a dozen occasions in which he displayed any human feeling or tenderness for anyone. He was polite, mild-mannered, formally correct in his dealings with me; he joked and chatted brightly at times, but his words seemed both hollow and empty. Even when he had come to accept and depend upon me, he remained astonishingly cold, unfeeling, affectionless. Of the dozen or so lads with whom he lived in prison, at least four exhibited great personal friendliness, warmth, and charm. As people, almost all of them were more immediately likable than he. Yet none had his power to move me to such compassion, and never did I feel its pull more strongly than when I left him.

He was entirely alone. It was this, as much as his lovelessness, that made him so forlorn a figure. He had no friends; his gang was a large, amorphous group under cover of which a small core of young criminals met to plan robberies. Its code was silence and absolute reserve between members; it offered no friendship and provided no security. Not once did Manuel mention the name of a single boy in the group for whom he ever felt the smallest personal regard. His family barely saw him; they knew nothing of his movements. Often they did not know where he was living, and they did not care what he was working at. His teachers scarcely remembered him. With the possible exception of two girls, his friendships hardly outlasted the week. His fellow prisoners despised and exploited him. He cut no ice anywhere. For all their ignorance and indifference, however, all of them saw the same Manuel. They fastened on the same traits, commented on the same weaknesses; they judged him by common standards and unanimously pronounced him a failure.

Still, there was a code and standard of values he acknowledged, even if it was confused, contradictory, and degenerate. It was partly a reaction against, partly an imitation of, the standards proclaimed by the films and the advertisements. Parties, dances, girls, gambling, drugs, drinking, fine clothes, the excitement of speed, the life of distraction. Manuel's "good life" was one poor man's version of *la dolce vita*. Since he did not possess the free time or the ample, unearned income necessary to its enjoyment, he adopted the only means available to an unskilled slum boy: he sought to acquire the things he wanted by stealing. He desired also companionship, love, above all the respect of his fellows. He never obtained them. He had no plans, no fixed policy, no capacity for foresight. Like a child, he was a creature of the immediate impulse; again like a child, he avenged disappointments with violence.

He was certainly not pushed into crime by want—if "want" means "grinding poverty." He was not pushed at all. The question, even in Manuel's eyes, was a good deal more complicated than that, and his own story is susceptible of different interpretations. He was a habitual thief, but he was not a professional. Until almost the end of the seven months I spent with him, he did not regard himself as a criminal at all, though he considered prison as unsurprising an institution as boarding school, and not much different.

There was a clear understanding between us from the start. He was free to say or not to say anything he wished. If there were subjects he did not want to talk about, he could drop them. If he wished to tell me his life story (which he did), he could do so in any way he chose. And he was free to put a stop to our meetings at will. In fact, he always had a clear idea of what he wanted to do and followed it out to the letter. He was immensely fluent and disliked interruption. Once I became accustomed to his style of speech, I hardly stopped him at all with questions. Occasionally, before a session started, I would go over some episode he had previously recounted, probing for inconsistencies or in search of more detail, and he was always more than ready to supply me with elaborate descriptions. Except at the end, when he came to matters of great emotional difficulty, he baulked only at full descriptions of gang robberies; even there he provided a good deal.

On my side, I made it clear that I was not attempting to influence him in any way. I had not come to guide him or to offer him advice or suggest how he should order his life. I was not even, in any ordinary or obvious sense, trying to help him. My only purpose was to listen and try to understand. Manuel, for his part, always thought of me as the man who was writing his biography, and lost no opportunity of letting the fact be known. Yet he did not tell me his story so much out of vanity as out of need: need to unburden himself, to have beside him a presence which would permit him to come to terms with himself. For more than half the time I knew him, he was as unaware of my presence as he was of the tape recorder beside him: he was talking to himself. He asked me to come to see him as often as I

could. And for more than seven months we saw each
other alone about twice a week, for two hours each
time.

I I

The form of this book, which is divided into five
parts, is that imposed upon it by the nature of the
material. In the first part I have presented Manuel as he
appeared to the legal authorities, the press, and the man
in the street: as a criminal. In this section I have
deliberately confined myself to the trial documents and
newspaper reports. The trial was not, of course, conducted in accordance with English or American law;
perhaps it is best described as a "trial by document."
There was no courtroom presided over by a judge and
devoted solely to Manuel's trial. Nor was the trial conducted in the presence of the accused, counsel, and
jury. On the contrary, accused and witnesses were
cited to appear individually in court to make their declarations, in the absence of any legal representation
whatever, to a public official seated at a table before
his typewriter. The court was a large room in which
other officials were similarly engaged while the judge
on duty sat in his corner, attending to his own business.
The public official asks no questions; he merely takes
down what is said to him, reads it over to the person
who has made the statement, and asks him to sign it as
correct.

The judge in charge of police investigations is also
responsible for giving the final verdict. He may examine

the accused and the witnesses, confront them with one another, ask them to explain contradictions or discrepancies in their testimony; he may visit the scene of the crime and ask the accused to reconstruct the events. But he must base his judgment exclusively on the written documents in the file (and the tape-recorded declarations, if there are any). When the case against the prisoner is complete, the documents become public and it is the turn of the accused to reply. His legal defense is conducted in similar fashion.

Manuel was thus "present" at his "trial" only when he was wanted—to make a statement, to be examined by the judge or confronted by a witness—or when he wished to make a statement on his own initiative. The rest of the time he remained in jail while his trial moved slowly forward without his participation or even knowledge. So the portrait of Manuel as the law sees him is necessarily his portrait as it emerges from a mass of documents. His lawyer and the judge may know a great deal "off the record"; they are free to make an estimate of his character and his veracity by seeing him in the flesh; they may listen to his taped depositions. But in the last resort they must base their decisions on the written evidence.

The press and the man in the street can go further. They can collect stories, interview witnesses, look at photographs, make use of private contacts and sources of information. In the first part of the book, however, I have used only what appeared in print.

In the second part, Manuel is presented as his fellow

prisoners saw him. To make that picture fully intel-
ligible, I have described the day-to-day prison life,
concentrating particularly on the situation of the juvenile offenders amongst whom Manuel was thrown. For
my material, I have drawn on hours of conversation
with the men and boys Manuel lived with in jail. I met
the boys and worked with them, talked to the man
Manuel worked with in his cell, chatted casually with
other prisoners. Contrary to popular belief, the poor and
the uneducated are frequently more articulate and
eloquent in speech than the middle-class beneficiaries
of a secondary-school education. If at any time I needed
detailed information on jail matters, none of the youths
or men with whom I talked was ever at a loss to provide
it. As readers will see, the conditions of prison life were
so primitive, so reminiscent of Dickens or even of
Fielding, and the need of aid so urgent and unremitting
that no one could afford the luxury of distrusting my
credentials.

The third part is devoted to Manuel's life up to his
sixteenth year. I have followed faithfully his own pres-
entation of his story, have maintained his own em-
phases, preserved his structure, and quoted his own
words at length when I thought they gave point to the
story. I have tried to reflect his outlook and record his
"facts." These are therefore his, not mine—unless I
specifically endorse them. I considered the possibility of
letting Manuel tell the whole of his story in his own
words, as if he were a second Holden Caulfield or
another lonely, long-distance runner. But he had too

little insight into his own life to permit this; the subtle ironies that were meaningful in *The Catcher in the Rye* lay too few and far between in the thickets of Manuel's real-life narrative to justify unvarnished inclusion here. So I have compromised. I have told the first fifteen years of his story in the third person, offering from time to time my own comments and interpretations. And then, in the fourth part, I have let Manuel give his own version of the last two years of his life, which are full of incident and excitement. Readers may detect a difference in tone between the earlier section, which is in the third person, and the later section, which is in the first. This is not merely due to a shift in point of view; it was caused by a number of other factors, which are discussed in the fifth and final part of the book.

This part deals with the character of Manuel's relationship to his life story and to me. In seven months this relationship changed considerably. For a boy of seventeen to sit down quietly at a table, while his trial for murder is proceeding, and tell a stranger for months on end the story of his life requires great courage. Men begin by telling their stories to gain relief; before long, they have opened their hearts. They end by re-enacting their lives. Between the end and the beginning there is a world of difference. The last part of the book, then, is the chronicle of that change. Its beginnings were scarcely perceptible; its growth was slow but unmistakable; its culmination painful, unforeseen and violent.

There is no doubt that I deeply affected Manuel both in the manner in which he projected his story and in the way he reacted to me. A man of different age, class, nation, and outlook would have seen him differently, heard a different story, interpreted what he heard in a different way. These things are radically subjective. I have tried to make allowance for this inevitable bias in two ways. First, I have provided alternative perspectives of him; I have shown what his family, his teachers, his fellow prisoners saw in him. I also attempted to check up on his story in various ways by visiting the schools he attended, meeting his teachers, seeing his home, visiting his haunts, talking to his lawyer. With one exception, however, I did not meet any of his family; nor did I see his mother. Though she had given her blessing to my activities and Manuel was anxious that I should meet her, I never did. All the same, I received reliable reports of the family's attitudes and comments about him, and I was left, finally, in no doubt about their attitude toward me.

The second method I adopted was to put myself as far as possible inside my own book as a character on the same footing as the others. I have deliberately made my own comments, written in a personal style, not hidden my private interests, tastes, or reactions. One cannot fairly judge a portrait without some chance to assess the quirks in the painter's vision.

I I I

My theme is what my title suggests it is: I have tried to produce a portrait of a particular kind of personality, not to provide a psychological or sociological analysis.

Or rather, I have offered a series of mirror images designed to reflect that personality, as seen by different kinds of men.

I have sought to tell a boy's story both for its intrinsic interest and for its value as a paradigm of the condition of the poor in a Latin-American society. In general, I have tried to present Manuel in a manner as innocent of professional interpretation as are the characters of the unemployed men and women who speak with such moving accents in the bare prose of Danilo Dolci's *Inchiesta a Palermo* or the members of Oscar Lewis's Mexican slum family in *The Children of Sánchez*. I have used no secret weapons to obtain my data—except ordinary friendliness, patience, and straightforward dealing—and there has been no question of payment for information. All the same, a portrait is an interpretation of a man, not a plaster model of him, and the reader is entitled to ask to what sorts of interpretation the author is most partial. Even professional innocence is, after all, a very relative matter; and a university teacher, of all people, cannot plausibly claim to see the world unhampered by academic blinkers, even if he is foolhardy enough to stray beyond his own well-mapped hunting grounds of philosophy and literature. Certainly, I cannot pretend to have learned nothing at all from books. Indeed, while I was writing this one, T. R. Fyvel's *Insecure Offenders* and a Chilean criminal's autobiography disguised as a novel, *El Río* by Alfredo Gómez Morel, taught me a great deal and gave me clues as to what to listen for. A third book, from which I would have profited if I had read it earlier, is Barbara Wootton's *Social Science and Social Pathology*. As it is, it reached me too late, except to relieve my anxiety that I might be nothing but a trespasser, ignorantly crossing cultivated ground in defiance of clearly posted warnings to keep out.

What, if anything, does *Manuel* show? That is anyone's guess. What it purports to do is simple enough: to show what a Chilean slum boy who is also a murderer is like—how he sees his own life, how he judges himself— and to ask what his prospects are. Perhaps it also throws some light on the extreme difficulty and complexity of the problems of juvenile crime, while pointing to the pitiable inadequacy of the present arrangements for dealing with them.

If, however, anyone chooses to read this book as an attack on a country's institutions, I hope he will remember that it was a prison governor's children who gave me the most help and encouragement at all times and that my freedom to wander unhindered through the wasteland of Chile's prisons was due to the safe conduct and co-operation of the authorities themselves. Let no one imagine that the men who work inside these prisons are unconcerned or blind to the institutions' faults. Quite the contrary: the public may be deaf to their voices, but they are far from silent.

I have altered the names of people in this book; I have also sought by small changes in detail to conceal the identities of one or two of the minor characters. The events themselves are authentic.

Part 1

⎍⎍⎍⎍⎍⎍⎍⎍⎍⎍⎍⎍⎍⎍⎍⎍⎍⎍⎍⎍⎍

The Crime and the Criminal

At her feet he bowed, he fell, he lay down: where he bowed, there he fell down dead. JUDGES V

I

|||| It happened in Valparaíso in 1962 between seven
and eight on an autumn evening in May; but it
could have happened in almost any provincial town
with a population of about half a million, a decaying
commerce, a Mediterranean climate, a sharp contrast in
standards of living, and a strong sense of exploitation on
the part of the poor.

To understand the details, you need a few elementary
facts about the city. Though Valparaíso is the largest
seaport in Chile and its second largest city, it is in frank
commercial decline. Wrapped in a blanket of the past,
the town seems to breathe the stale air of the retired
pensioner, living in reduced circumstances, obedient to
old conventions, hiding from the winds of change: the
very tempo of its life suggests, by its absence, a vigor
that has now forever left it. The style of architecture of
its commercial buildings, the English names of its foreign firms, its public monuments and private tomb-
stones speak to its present inhabitants, if they care to
listen, of a vanished age; its wooden houses, which once
stood proud and dignified in what were smart residen-
tial areas on the city's many hills overlooking the spa-
cious bay, have become flyblown tenements or run-
down public buildings; its narrow, winding streets now
lead all too often to complicated beehives of photogenic
slums. The very elevators in the city's banks and commercial buildings—slow, noisy, old-fashioned cages
with iron gates—and the slow, dangerous, inefficient
"funiculars" that connect the town with the surrounding

hills seem a fitting symbol of its life: sluggish, precarious, picturesque, and fatal. Still, Valparaíso can boast a public library and a cathedral, set in a large, tree-sheltered central plaza; a fine old Spanish baroque church, now encroached upon by a dock area of dubious reputation; no less than three universities; a stock exchange, a fair number of commercial firms, a custom-house, law courts, and a jail.

The rich have moved elsewhere. Some have gone inland to the capital; some have merely moved a few miles up the coast, to the neighboring dormitory town of Viña del Mar, whose handsome casino, beaches, restaurants, and blocks of luxury apartments attract a brisk tourist trade in summer and have even lured world football teams to play in its vast, new stadium. Indeed, an enterprising mayor has gone to considerable trouble to put the city on the map: unlike his predecessor, now in hiding in Venezuela, wanted for fraud. Tourist brochures celebrate the town as the Pearl of the Pacific; travel agencies in foreign capitals put out posters of the city's bridges, spanning in majestic arches a riverbed; American tourists and sailors from foreign ships take their Leica color photographs. But the brochures do not mention, and the tourists do not notice, that the city's abandoned children sleep under the bridges and that the riverbed, which has been for years a potent source of mosquitoes in summer, is also the natural home of crime. The mosquitoes have been eliminated: they were bad for the tourist trade. The crime remains. Viña and Valparaíso, though run by different municipalities and reflecting different interests, are still intimately linked. The bulk of the commerce of the area is still conducted in Valparaíso: to it the commercial and professional population travels from Viña by bus, train, or car every day. A brief, comfortable, and easy journey of some twenty minutes to lawyer's office or business firm.

One such firm, plumb in the commercial center of the city, not a stone's throw away from the Stock Exchange, overlooked by the grandiose façade of the Bank of London and South America, and protected by the heraldic shield of the British Consulate General, is the Consorcio Italiano. It occupies the first two floors of a large, six-story building; the offices on the other floors are rented out to smaller firms, one-man businesses, and individual professional men.

About a quarter to seven in the evening of Monday, May 7, Juan Calderón, the elevator man, took two men up to the fourth floor. The older man looked like a lawyer; the younger man, his client. They went a bare couple of yards across the passage to the office of an elderly lawyer, Enrique Mercier, but did not go in. Instead, Mercier came to the door and chatted for a moment or two with them there. They then left. Calderón hardly had time to turn on the corridor lights before they asked to be taken down again to the first floor. They could not have been in the building five minutes.

Very soon afterwards, Calderón had another summons from the fourth floor. He went up again and this time saw Mercier standing at the elevator gates. The lawyer apologized for ringing; it was a mistake. The two

men talked for a minute or two, pointlessly, about the
passage lights; without getting out of the elevator,
Calderón explained how to work them. During this conversation he noticed a young man standing behind Mercier, by the closed office door. He looked poor; wore a
pullover without a jacket and a pair of dark gray trousers. Calderón looked at him with interest. He had not
seen him before. The boy dropped his eyes and gave the
impression that he was trying to avoid being seen. He
carried a smallish, brown paper parcel which he was
holding rather awkwardly in front of him with both
hands. Calderón stayed long enough to see Mercier
usher him, without speaking, into his office and shut the
door. It was now almost seven o'clock. The elevator
man's working day was over. He made his last trip
down, washed, and left the building. He met a friend,
by arrangement, for a drink and the two went on to a
well-known and much patronized brothel in the port
area, where they stayed until the early hours of the
morning.

If the elevator man's cares were thus easily cast aside
after seven, those of Victor Ramírez, the caretaker of
the Consorcio Italiano building, were only just beginning. His job was to see that the doors of the offices were
properly locked and the lights turned out once their
occupants had left for home. At a quarter to eight, he
was still waiting to complete this part of his job when
the young son of the general manager of the Consorcio
Italiano emerged from the building and made off in the
direction of his car. The caretaker, as was his custom,

caught up with him and they chatted for a few minutes. As Ramírez stood looking up at the building from the street, the lights of three windows on the fifth floor, which belonged to the offices of Olivari and Company —the only ones apparently still burning—went out. That, however, did not mean that there were no offices still in use. The general manager of the Consorcio Italiano was still in his indoor office on the first floor, and some of the windows which looked out onto the street—like Mercier's, for instance—had thick blinds that did not let the light through: they functioned like blackout curtains. The caretaker decided to give the tenants a bit longer. In the meantime, he went out for a cup of tea.

Ten minutes later, when he glanced up again at the building from street level, he was surprised to see a light burning in Mercier's office on the fourth floor. It had certainly not been visible earlier, and he thought it odd that Mercier should have forgotten to turn his lights out before leaving; the lawyer had never failed to do so in the past. It was even more surprising that he should still be there, as he normally left well before this time. It was now almost eight o'clock. So the caretaker entered the building and took the elevator up to Mercier's office. As he was about to reach the second floor, he heard footsteps—someone was coming down the stairs; at the same moment, Señor Olivari called up to him from the first. So Ramírez stopped the elevator and came down on foot to speak to him. The conversation did not last more than a moment or two; the caretaker then continued his journey in the elevator to Mercier's office. He had thought it strange that the lawyer should still be there at this hour, with all the lights on. It seemed even stranger that Mercier did not call down to him not to bother coming up; this was the lawyer's invariable practice when he worked late.

By the time Ramírez reached the fourth floor, surprise had turned to suspicion. He did not need to open the gate to see through the elevator bars that the door of Mercier's office was ajar and the light on. He called out repeatedly, but received no answer. Feeling certain that something was wrong, he took the elevator down again to the first floor and asked the porter of the Consorcio Italiano to come with him. They got out of the elevator on the fourth floor and peered rather gingerly through the door of Mercier's office. What they caught sight of on the floor was Mercier's body: or, more exactly, his bare legs. As they strained to get a better view, they saw that he was wearing no trousers or underpants. He was clad only in a shirt, tie, socks, and a pair of shoes. They did not go in. Ramírez told the porter to stay where he was, on guard outside the door, while he went on up to the fifth and sixth floors to see if anyone was hiding there. He found no one. He called the police.

The lawyer's office, which the caretaker and his assistant had a little earlier that evening not dared to enter, now became the scene of intense police activity. In itself, the office was ordinary enough. Frowsty, conventional, down at heel, it reflected faithfully the very moderate professional success of its occupant as well as his social pretensions. Its furnishings could hardly have been duller or more respectable: desk and swivel chair, two small stands for telephone and typewriter, a safe, two worn black leather armchairs, a sofa, pictures —apart from a few twentieth-century anachronisms, it could well have served as a "set" for a solicitor's office near a cathedral close in Trollope. There was a waiting room adjoining it, furnished in much the same style.

That night the police found the tenant lying unconscious, wedged between two armchairs, his head badly battered and his arms and eyes bruised. On a rucked-up rug beside him lay his scarf and overcoat. On the chair to his right lay his hat, his jacket, and his trousers; on the chair to his left, his cardigan, apart. Beyond the desk, in the opposite corner, on the same side of the room as the sofa, was the safe—half-open; in the opposite corner, a telephone stand. A foot away stood an opened bottle of brandy. A little distance off lay a stone, wrapped in bloodstained brown paper—the kind used for cement bags. It was a big stone weighing nearly five pounds, and it looked as if it had been worn smooth and clean by water. At the foot of the sofa, on the floor, were a crushed newspaper, a piece of string, and a pair of underpants. There were several stains on the floor, but there were no signs of a struggle.

Mercier never regained consciousness and died before morning. The subsequent autopsy confirmed what most people present in that room must by now have taken for granted. The victim, while sitting or crouching beneath his assailant, had been battered to death from the back with a blunt instrument. Some of the blows had been dealt after he had already fallen; he had attempted to defend himself with his hands, but had been struck on them. He had a badly bruised right eye, and he must have been kicked in the leg. He had been struck at least four times. He was also a habitual passive pederast. Mercier had apparently invited his murderer in.

A day elapsed following Mercier's death on the morning of the eighth before the news reached the public. By Wednesday, however, the papers were busy making hay while the sun shone. It was shining, for them, very brightly indeed. The murder had been committed in the very center of the commercial section of the city, the area of the tourist postcards and the picturesque nineteenth-century buildings; the victim had been well known in business and legal circles; he had married into a family that had meant something in the life of the city a hundred years ago and still held a place in good Chilean society. Thus his funeral, conducted by the Archbishop in the cathedral that looked out on the main plaza, was fully reported in the press, and pictures of the Mercier family vault, in the heavy imposing style of the last century, were prominently displayed in the papers. Even so, the respectable press was not able to conceal entirely the more doubtful aspects of Mercier's character, and the popular papers made no effort to do so. It was not long before the trickle of hints and rumors became a flood.

The statements of the early witnesses made this inevitable. A stone wrapped in brown paper had robbed Mercier of his life; but the press publicity attendant on the police inquiry went further: it destroyed his reputation. It turned out that Mercier's proclivities were an open secret. They were by no means unknown to many of the people who worked in the office block; the general manager of the Consorcio Italiano was later to depose that there had been complaints about the visitors Mercier entertained in his office and that he had asked the lawyer to move. It was left, however, to the elevator-man and the caretaker to provide the police with the most detailed information concerning Mercier's visitors. Both these men had sharp eyes and a keen nose for scandal and were in no doubt about the purpose of the visits of the young men whom they observed in the late afternoons scurrying like rabbits up the stairs to the fourth-floor office. Both had kept tabs on the lawyer's most recent and assiduous visitors; on two in particular. One was a young man of twenty-six. They knew his name. He had been employed the previous year by Mercier to clean the windows of his office, and had since then been seen leaving "nearly every evening with the lawyer after office hours, carrying his briefcase." The other, young and dark-skinned, had appeared on the scene much more recently; neither caretaker nor elevator man knew who he was. The caretaker, however, had met him twice on the stairs either going to or coming from Mercier's office and had seen him last on the Thursday before the crime. He remembered the

occasion well, as they had had an altercation. He had
said to the young man: "What nice fresh meat Don
Enrique has nowadays!" The young man had lost his
temper, replied that he had as much right to be defended by a lawyer as anyone else, and warned the
caretaker to watch his tongue. The caretaker, by way of
retort, had threatened to hit the young man. He recol-
lected also that on that Thursday evening both young
men had almost simultaneously called on Mercier; the
dark young man had left about five minutes after the
other arrived.

The caretaker gave a detailed and careful description of this man. It was as follows: age about twenty-
two; height about five foot five inches (he actually said:
"one meter sixty-five centimeters—a standard way of
describing the height of a small man in Chile); dark-
skinned; with black hair, combed back; round face;
smooth shiny skin—the sort you don't have to shave;
neither fat nor thin. The caretaker had not seen him the
Monday of the crime, but he had previously seen him
wearing a pair of dark gray trousers with a stitched-
up tear on the right side of the seat, and a black
high-necked sweater. He wore no jacket. The description tallied well with that given by the elevator man of
the young man he had seen standing outside Mercier's
shut office door a little before seven on the evening of
the Monday. He gave the same guess as to height;
added that the young man had a dark face—with
smooth skin, the kind you do not need to shave; black,
slightly wavy hair. That Monday he was wearing a dark

purple, long-sleeved, high-necked sweater and dark gray trousers. He was twenty or twenty-one.

The first man was quickly rounded up and brought in for questioning. His name was Claudio Ramos. He admitted that he knew Mercier, that he had frequently had relations with him; he gave a long and detailed account of the Thursday evening when he had been in the office, but emphatically denied that he had seen the lawyer since.

He had originally met Mercier while he was working in the house of a man called Rocco Pozzi. He had been invited to attend Pozzi's name-day celebration. The occasion could therefore be precisely dated as August 26, 1961. Mercier had evidently taken a fancy to him, as he had asked him to come the following Saturday to clean the windows of his office. He went and was given one thousand pesos (one dollar) for his services. He was then asked to return the following Tuesday at seven in the evening to help tidy up the office papers. It was on this occasion that Mercier made overtures toward him. They were very frank and obvious. Since Ramos raised no objection, they had relations. For this service, which he was to repeat at regular intervals throughout this and the following year until three weeks before Mercier's death, Ramos usually received two hundred pesos, certainly never more than two hundred and fifty: sufficient for a single ticket for the gallery of a popular cinema in town—which is just what he used it for.

Toward the end of September Ramos became very ill and was sent to hospital. He was discharged in November due to the acute shortage of bed space, and he returned home. Throughout December he was still too unwell to work. During this time Mercier went round to his home to see him three times. By mid-January Ramos was back at work. He then continued his visits twice monthly to Mercier's office and resumed his sexual relations with him. After Good Friday (April 20), however, Mercier always found excuses for not having sexual dealings with him; he was not feeling well or he was too tired or he had to go off to Quillota. Ramos began to suspect that he had found a new boyfriend.

He gave the following account of their meeting on the Thursday before Mercier's death. Immediately on arrival he was asked to open a bottle of brandy, while Mercier went to see someone who was sitting in the waiting room, reading the evening paper. After getting rid of his visitor fairly quickly, Mercier returned, offered Ramos a glass of brandy, took one himself, and started talking about the man in the waiting room, whom he referred to as a "dark chap" (*un moreno*). Ramos himself did not get a chance to see him, but suspected that he must be the new boyfriend. Mercier and Ramos left the office together, but parted once they reached the street. Ramos insisted he never saw Mercier alive again.

Everything now seemed to point to the "dark" young man, who kept cropping up in the testimony of witnesses. He had been seen by the caretaker on the Thursday; he was known to have been in Mercier's office at the same time as Ramos, even though Ramos had not actually seen him; he had been referred to by the lawyer as "dark"; and he had been seen again on the fatal Monday in the evening, a little before seven, carrying a brown paper parcel in both hands. The descriptions all tallied. The papers published an "identi-kit" portrait of him; there were hints of a significant link between the mysterious visitors Calderón had taken up in the elevator (who had not come forward or been identified) and Mercier's death; there were even suggestions that the crime was inspired, not by robbery, but by jealousy or revenge on the part of a homosexual ring said to be operating in the city. Hundreds of suspects were rounded up by the police for questioning. Fishermen in particular were favorite quarry, for the stains on the paper the stone had been wrapped in turned out to be those of fish. The papers claimed that rich men in sleek limousines waited at nightfall to pick young fishermen up as they returned from work along the esplanade. It was evident that press and radio were "going to town."

The police, meanwhile, were asking other, more prosaic questions. If the murderer's motive had been robbery, how much had he taken? How much had he found in the safe? How much money was Mercier carrying? The lawyer had the reputation, among his friends and family, of being a very reserved man. No one volunteered any suggestion as to how much there might have been in the safe, but his wife deposed that he was in the habit of going about with quite large sums of money in his wallet—as much as fifty escudos (fifty dollars). The only known facts, however, were that the safe had been opened and that his wallet had disappeared.

Who was the dark young man? What was his motive? Radio and press demanded, and the police promised, a speedy solution to these intriguing questions. The public waited eagerly for the criminal to be caught and brought to justice. For two days nothing happened.

I I

Just as the shops were opening in Limache, an inland country town about forty miles outside Valparaíso, on Friday, May 11, a young policeman by the name of Hugo Garrido entered the shoeshop of a man he had known since his schooldays. Garrido wanted him to cash a check for fifty escudos. The owner of the shop, Cesar Palma, agreed to do so at once. The check, which was dated the previous day, was drawn on the same bank in which Palma had his account, and he was due to deposit his checks there a little later that same morning. As the bearer's name had been left blank on the check, Palma asked the policeman to fill in his own name and endorse it on the back. Garrido did so; Palma then went to the till and gave him five notes of ten escudos each. The policeman thanked him briefly and left. He walked to the corner, where a young boy of sixteen was waiting for him, and handed all the money to him. This boy, whose name was Carlos López, went at once into a nearby bank to change one of the notes into smaller denominations and returned to the policeman, to whom he gave four escudos. The two then parted.

Garrido had been doing the boy a favor. Carlos's half-brother, Francisco, was his personal friend; they were in the police force together. It was true that Francisco had recently been transferred to the dock area in Valparaíso, but he had kept his house in Limache and he and Garrido often met for supper there during the weekends. The previous evening Carlos, whom Garrido had met accidentally on the street, had brought him sad news. His brother, he said, had been arrested for debt and had sent him (Carlos) posthaste to Limache with a check his brother had obtained from a friend. Carlos was supposed to change it for him and pay his debts. Could Garrido please oblige? The policeman did not for a moment doubt the story. Francisco was always running into debt; in fact, only a month earlier, when Garrido had last seen the brothers together in Limache at their home, he had himself paid a small bill of four escudos for Francisco. Now Garrido promised to get the check cashed the following morning when the shops opened; and Carlos was able to pay back that small debt on his brother's behalf.

Meanwhile, Cesar Palma had gone off to the Banco Sud Americano de Quillota to make his deposit. Garrido's check was questioned immediately. Palma was told that the check was not only forged, it belonged to a man whose funds were frozen, for he was dead. His

name was Enrique Mercier. Astonished, Palma wasted
no time in going around to Garrido's home while the
policeman was there having lunch, to demand an
explanation. He then went to report the matter to the
police.

The authorities acted at once. Francisco Sánchez,
who had not been arrested for debt at all, was sum-
moned to Limache from Valparaíso, where he was on
duty, and informed by Garrido of what his brother had
done. Francisco was then required to go with Garrido to
search the Sánchez house in Limache—where Francisco
had so often entertained his friend in the past. Carlos,
of course, was not there.

It was now Francisco's turn to be put on the spot.
Since his marriage, some months earlier, he had lost
touch with his brother and did not know what work he
had or even where he lived. By chance, however, on his
rounds in the dock area the previous week he had met
Carlos outside the Cachás Grandes Café, a well-known
hangout for thieves. His younger brother had presented
him on that occasion with the cancelled draft of a bill
for furniture Francisco had run up when he had
married. Francisco was, naturally enough, grateful to
Carlos for his generosity in paying it, but it had not occurred to him to wonder how his brother, who was
only sixteen, could afford to meet such an obligation.

With the help of two photographs Francisco provided, the police decided to search the hotels of the
dock area for Carlos. A little before midnight, in a cheap
hotel not twenty yards from the Cachás Grandes Café,

where his brother had last seen him, they discovered the boy in bed with a young girl. When he was searched, they found on him a check for eighty escudos, dated May 9. It was drawn on the Banco Sud Americano de Quillota, had the number following that of the check cashed by the Limache shopkeeper that same day, but it was filled in and signed by a different hand.

The boy and girl were taken in for questioning. They were thoroughly frightened. Carlos was, after all, only sixteen, and he was appalled at being told that he was mixed up in murder. Only too anxious to clear himself of any suggestion of being implicated in so grave a matter, he leaned over backwards to give the police a full account of his movements since the day of the crime. He had come to Valparaíso in the first week of April and had soon taken to patronizing the Cachás Grandes Café in the dock area. There, he said, toward the end of the month he had met a boy called Cristián Garcés. They had met casually one day when Cristián had come up to Carlos to ask for a cigarette, and they had become friendly. They usually met in the Cachás Grandes Café when he was with his girl friend, with whom Cristián had also become friendly. Cristián had told them that he had been thrown out of his parents' home, and now spent the nights sometimes at his girl friend's house in a poor suburb of Viña known as Forestal Alto, sometimes in a disused railway coach in Bellavista Station. At about half past four in the afternoon of Tuesday, May 8, Carlos had bumped into Cristián again outside the Cachás Grandes Café. This

time Carlos was surprised to see his friend wearing
dark glasses and dressed from top to toe in new
clothes—blue jeans, flashy white pullover with black
stripes, clean white shirt, and dark blue tie. Conspira-
torially, Cristián had asked him to join him in the
"Gents." There he had produced a checkbook, torn out
two checks on the Banco Sud Americano de Quillota,
and given them to Carlos as a present. He said he
wanted Carlos to buy new clothes. Cristián had made
up with his parents, no longer needed the money the
checks represented, and pressed them on his friend. He
said if Carlos did not take them he would simply tear
them up. Carlos had accepted them with thanks, and
the boys had then parted. He had not seen Cristián
since. Of the two checks he was so unexpectedly given,
one he filled in at once; that evening he went off to
Limache, where he had friends, to cash it. He confirmed
Garrido's story and related in detail what he had spent
the money on—mainly presents for his girl friend. On
his return to Valparaíso at midday, he had gone in
search of Celia to give her the stockings he had bought
for her, and to invite her to lunch. They then went on to
a three-feature-film show in a popular cinema, from
which they came out at eight in the evening. Feeling
hungry, they went for a bite to a nearby snack bar and
had hot dogs. After going dancing at a local nightclub
known as the Turin Bar, they ended the evening
together at the Hotel Marina, at 10:30 p.m., a few doors
from the Cachás Grandes, where they had started.
Carlos paid the hotel in advance, registering under his

brother's name, and gave Celia ten escudos to sleep with him. The rest of the money went on the hotel bill and on meals.

The girl was also called upon to make a statement. She appears in the documents as Celia Rojas; age, fifteen; civil status, married. She had met Carlos López and Cristián Garcés about a month earlier at the Cachás Grandes, where "you meet women like me." She liked them both, and always treated them to drinks or let herself be treated to them whenever they happened to meet in the café. Cristián had told her that he had run away from home, but that his family was very well off, "little less than millionaires." She, too, had her own story to tell. "Sometime ago, on Wednesday the ninth I think it was, Garcés arrived at about 2:30 in the afternoon at the Cachás Grandes Café with a check for López, which he filled in there and then and handed to me. He said he was now back at home and no longer needed to make use of the checks he had taken from his father. He said this in such a natural way that I automatically believed him; he had always said his parents were rich people. I was pulled in that day on suspicion, but released the following day. On the day I got out I gave López the check and arranged to meet him on Friday afternoon (May 11). We had drinks together in the Turin Bar, and I got completely drunk. That night López and I went to bed together in the Hotel Marina. Sometime after that—I don't remember what time—we were arrested. It was only then that I learned that the check I had hidden the first time I was pulled

in and later given to López came from the murdered
man's checkbook. I had no idea."

The police were soon satisfied that this youthful pair
had nothing to do with the murder. They were after
Cristián Garcés, the boy in blue jeans and striped
pullover, who had given Carlos the checks. But how to
find him? They searched their records to see whether
any Cristián Garcés had been arrested recently. A
Cristián Nidolfson had been picked up on suspicion a
day before the crime; but he had been let out the
following morning, and had given a false address. So
the clue led nowhere. The only thing for it was to hunt
among the disused railway coaches in Bellavista
Station, the favorite haunt of abandoned children
since the sewers of the nearby plaza had been sealed
off. The police also set out to scour the poor suburb of
Viña where López had said Cristián's girl friend lived.
By seven in the morning, a tousled youth had been
found asleep in an adobe hut owned by a family called
Gamonal. Beside the bed lay Mercier's checkbook,
watch, and wallet. The wallet still contained the
lawyer's identity card and an expired membership
card for the Viña Casino. The youth was arrested immediately.

With him to the police station went four of the other
occupants of the shack: José Gamonal, fifty-four, municipal employee in Viña; the woman who lived with
him as his wife, Waldemira Araya, forty-eight; her
eldest daughter, Rosa Marcelina Araya, nineteen, domestic servant; and Gamonal and Waldemira's

daughter, Judith Gamonal, fifteen, who was still at school. Señor Gamonal knew the boy as Cristián Nicholls; his wife and Judith called him Cristián Garcés. Only Rosa Marcelina Araya, the first member of the family to have met him—a month previously at a carnival—knew his real name: Manuel Garcés. He had come round once or twice after their first meeting, but she had not been in and he had subsequently become friends with her younger half-sister. They had lost track of him, however, until May 7, when he had turned up unexpectedly at about ten in the evening and asked for a bed for the night. He had had a row with his parents and could not return home. So he had stayed until he had been arrested a few days later. None of the family had noticed anything unusual in his behavior. Gamonal's wife had even discussed the murder with him; he had made no particular comment and always appeared calm and cheerful. They knew nothing much about him but had had no objection to their fifteen-year-old daughter becoming his "official" girl friend.

What happened between seven in the morning, when the police entered the Gamonal home, and eleven, when the press were informed that Mercier's murderer had been caught and had made a full confession, does not, of course, appear in the documents. But Manuel Garcés now appeared before the public in person, a captive of justice and the press, to be photographed, cross-questioned, and endlessly discussed. The gist of his confession was communicated to the reporters; for about a week Manuel remained headline news, the

subject of animated private and public argument. The
popular press wrote articles about his background; even
the archbishop who had buried Mercier made an allu-
sion in an interview to the crime.

In retrospect, knowing what I now know, I find it
hard to recapture the extraordinary effect Manuel
Garcés' personality and confession had on the men in
charge of the case and, through the publicity given by
press and radio, on the public at large. It was both
disconcerting and ambiguous. The photographs in the
popular press presented a slight, dark, strikingly good-
looking youth with big, tender eyes, dressed in blue
jeans and large, loose white sweater with flashy black
stripes. Due chiefly to the statements made by the
young men who had been paid, and paid pathetically
little, by the dead man for their sexual services, popular
revulsion against the victim was at its height. The
accounts of a boy of seventeen who had been thrown
out of his home, who was said to have been living in
disused railway coaches, sleeping in adobe huts among
people who had casually befriended him and hardly
knew him, produced a spontaneous reaction of sympathy in his favor. There was a feeling, vague and
inarticulate but insistent, that the real victim was the
accused boy. At the same time there was something
disconcerting about the pictures and their accompany-
ing texts: this young man might be, indeed he obviously
was, extremely poor; his situation was hopeless; yet he
appeared to be posing before the photographers. It was
not just that he was not sorry to be the center of public

attention; he seemed almost to be asserting his right to
it—as if he thought that the sensation of the moment
made him the hero of the hour. This image of the "little
boy lost" was not at all what had been expected; the
public was jolted by the strange gap between the details
of a brutal crime and the personality of this boy, who
admitted his guilt with what appeared to be a certain
smugness.

I I I

These mixed feelings were not made any less confused by the text of the confession. It read as follows:

I met this man about three weeks ago. I happened to
be walking down the street outside the building of the
Consorcio Italiano, where he has his office, when he
spoke to me. "Look, George," he said, "don't you
remember me?" (*Oye, Jorge, ¿no te acuerdas de mí?*)
"No, señor," I replied.

Then he said to me: "I am a lawyer: let's go up to my
office. It's nothing to do with the caretaker; he can't do
anything. I pay the rent, and I can do as I like there; it's
just as if I were in my own home. I can stay there until
ten o'clock at night, if I want."

I stayed in his office till about a quarter to eight,
talking about hundreds of different things. I arranged to
go back there again the following day at eight. So I
went, and again we just talked. He offered me a glass of
brandy and some cigarettes. I was still there when we
heard someone coming, so he got me to go into the next

room. When I left he told me to come back two days later—I didn't see his friend's face. I went on various occasions after that to see him, but he never asked me to have sexual relations with him then. He gave me a hundred or two hundred pesos each time I went: once he gave me a thousand pesos (a dollar). The next to last time I saw him he made it perfectly clear that he wanted us to have sexual relations. He said so straight out—adding, "even if only once." I said I would come back next day—it was then the Friday before the crime; but I didn't go on Saturday. Instead, I thought of going on Monday evening. As I considered he was stringing me along with his offers of money and work, I decided to go to the fishermen's creek, which is called San Mateo, to get a stone from the seashore. I picked an ordinary-sized one I saw nearby, wrapped it up in a piece of brown paper used for carrying cement, and tucked it under my right arm. Then I walked along the bus route to where the streets of the dock area begin, and left the packet with a street vendor there; I don't know his name. I had wrapped it up in newspaper and tied it with string.

After walking away—it was about five to seven—I bumped into a friend who invited me to have a beer with him. I knew him as El Choche. I had a Coca-Cola with him in the Cachás Grandes Café; we left about ten past seven. I then went back to the stand where I had left the stone and asked the boy for it. He told me to get it from under the stand, where I had left it.

I then took it with me to the Consorcio Italiano. The

door of the building was open, so I walked in and climbed the stairs to the fourth floor. No one saw me. When I reached Mercier's office, the door was closed, but the shutters were open and I could see a light and Mercier sitting at his desk.

He heard me tap on the pane, looked up, and recognized me. Then he opened up for me, and told me to go to the next room, as he was still working, and his friend might call. The same thing had happened on previous occasions, so I wasn't surprised. Mercier gave me a chair in the office next door, put an ashtray beside me, and lit me a cigarette. He asked me what I had in my package. I told him it was a magneto. As I had told him I used to work as a mechanic, he found this answer quite satisfactory. I had been there about five minutes when he came back for the ashtray. He returned again later and ushered me into the office where he had been working. So I took the package with the stone in it with me and followed him in. My idea was to threaten him into giving me money, or hit him—though not very hard. I did not think he would report the matter to the police. Besides, I knew his address in Viña: if anything happened, I could go and tell them what had been happening between us in his office. Mercier then told me that we should do what up to now we had never done together before. I asked him if he had found me a job or was going to give me any money. He answered that he did not have any work for me and that he couldn't give me any money, as he had very little on him and what he had he needed to buy odds and ends— stamps, application forms, things like that. Then he took off his jacket and cardigan, and put two checkbooks and his wristwatch on top of the desk. We had already agreed to have sexual relations—we had not had them before, because it had never been possible. He had always been too busy, or someone had called up from home telling him to get back early. Dressed only in his shirt, tie, socks, and shoes, he leaned on the right arm of the sofa, ready for the sexual act. As he was standing like this, it passed through my mind that Mercier was just stringing me along: he wouldn't give me any cash, and he was not going to look for a job for me. This is what passed through my mind as I started to have sexual relations with him: he kept pressing me to "come." So I stopped, picked up the package, which was lying at our feet, and took off the newspaper wrapping. Mercier wanted to turn round, but I got him to keep his eyes down by telling him not to look yet, as I was going to show him something he would like. I took the stone in both hands—it was still wrapped in the cement paper—and hit him with it twice on the back of the head, as he stood bent over in the position I have already mentioned. He groaned, and I think he said something like "You've given me quite a blow, Jote"—or "Jorge" (*"Me pegaste fuerte, Jote"—o "Jorge"*). He kept on muttering things, but I could not hear him properly. He fell—half on the sofa, half on the floor. After the first blow I gave him, he tried to get up, so I gave him a second blow on the head. He tried to defend himself, but he wasn't able to do so. I didn't struggle with him. After stunning him, I went through his cardigan pockets, but found nothing. In his jacket I found a key ring, some small keys, and a quantity of small change—about five hundred pesos. I kept the keys and the money. I looked at the keys first and saw that the biggest might belong to the safe. I went over to it and as I passed the desk I pocketed the two checkbooks and the watch. I wasn't interested in the pen, which was also on top of the desk, so I left that. Before that, I had taken Mercier's wallet, also from his jacket pocket, and slipped it in my own pocket. I opened the safe but it contained only papers. I tried to open the small boxes inside the safe as well, but I couldn't find the right key. I tried them, but it was no good. I left the safe open, took the package and Mercier's overcoat, one under each arm, and went off, leaving the door open. When I had gone three or four steps down the stairs, I heard Mercier moaning—something like "Don Guillermo"; there were also sounds of voices in the building. The elevator was on the first or second floor. I got frightened and went back to the office, and as Mercier was still groaning and moaning, I gave him another blow on the head with the stone. He was lying as I had left him: half on the sofa, half on the floor. I threw the stone on the floor and chucked away the overcoat as well. Then I went over to the desk and rifled that, but found nothing. So I left without shutting the door and went down the stairs as fast as I could. Before giving him the final blow, I gagged him with his underpants. He had his mouth shut, so I could not fasten them properly: I just tied a knot in them.

As I was going down the stairs, I heard the elevator coming up and I called out loudly: "Don Guillermo, someone wants you upstairs." I presumed this was the caretaker's name. I did not see him, but I imagined it was him. I then continued down the stairs. When I got to the bottom, I heard people talking. I became desperate. I hunted in my pockets for the small key which opened the gate at the rear of the building. I found it, unlocked the gate, and left that way.

After that, I lit a cigarette and walked off quickly; I didn't run. I kept thinking I wished I had not hit him so hard. I continued walking—it was about ten minutes to eight by Mercier's watch—until I reached the Port Station. At eight I got in the train, and waited for it to go. But by ten past eight I changed my mind, got out of the train, and started walking along the Costanera towards Barón. On the way I asked a policeman the time; he told me it was about a quarter past eight. I had forgotten I was wearing Mercier's watch. I went on walking, then threw the key ring into the sea. I went on toward Bellavista. From there I crossed over to Errázuriz as far as Barón. Outside the Gas Company I took a blue or green bus to Viña. I got off at the Plaza de Viña and walked to Quillota Bridge, then on to the point in Calle Arlegui where the Forestal buses start climbing up the hill. Here I went down into the riverbed, where I counted the money in the wallet. There were about twelve thousand pesos (twelve dollars)—two five-thousand-peso notes, the rest in ten- and hundred-peso notes. I had lain down on the ground, sheltered by a wall, to do this; by the light of some street lamps I could see the time. I noticed that the watch was a Longines. I also counted the checks in the checkbooks. I think there were twenty-three on the Edwards Bank and five or six on the Banco Sud Americano. Later I took an 11 bus, as I thought of going to my girl friend's house. This was the first time I had ever stayed the night there. I asked her and her mother to let me stay; I said I had a week off. It was now about ten o'clock. I had a bed to myself there. Next day I went back to Valparaíso. I intended to change my clothes, as I was wearing a pair of gray pants which were torn in the seat, and a gray jersey, and I was frightened someone might recognize me. I only took two hundred pesos and the checkbooks with me to town. In Valparaíso I bumped into Carlos López, whom I had known before and with whom I used to have drinks in the Cachás Grandes Café. I rather liked him; he was different from the other boys. (Manuel was to amplify this later, in these words: "Besides, we had done a job together a few days earlier. This consisted in my getting hold of a drunk, whom we saw on Quillota Bridge [one of the bridges in Viña, beneath which abandoned children lived], by the neck, while one of the others who was with us—I don't know his name—took about twelve hundred pesos from his pockets. There were two others with us: 'Screwball' and this fellow I've mentioned. He's about my build, a bit thinner, I should say. Then we ran off and spent the money in the Mokambo Café"—barely a hundred yards away. López confirmed this story; so eventually did "Screwball," who turned out to be a clubfooted boy of sixteen. His father, a professional thief, hated him, considered him a police informer, and had turned him out of his home. The boy made a living taking American sailors off to brothels and robbing them there. On this occasion he had hidden while the assault was on for fear of getting mixed up in it, but he joined the boys afterwards in the Mokambo for coffee.)

We then left there, and went on to a soda fountain, the Metropole. I changed my clothes in the lavatory there and put on what I am wearing now. I had collected these clothes from the street vendor I mentioned earlier, who had kept them for me under his stand. In the Cachás Grandes I gave López two checks: I just tore them out of the checkbooks. I didn't write anything in them: they were blank. (The vendor, who was nineteen, was to tell a slightly different story: he said that Manuel had appeared in new clothes, which he described correctly, and that he had made jokes about where the money had come from to pay for them. He had also been shown a gold watch, two checkbooks, and a quantity of money.)

I returned to my girl friend's house, taking my old clothes with me in a bag I bought especially for that purpose. I had lunch there and left afterwards. That night we went to the movies, my girl friend, her mother, and I. We saw *Aladdin* and *Back Street* in the Municipal Theater. No, I am wrong: the second film was *The Phantom of the Opera*. The next day I went to Valparaíso again and met a girl I was friendly with, Celia, in a bar. I gave her a check for eighty escudos. I did this out of pure kindness; she had been very good to me when I had no money. I told her to get the check changed and to make some arrangement with López. (Manuel was to amplify his reasons later, in these words: "I did this because Celia told me that she had seen Carlos the night before, drinking and getting through a lot of money, which made me think that he had blown all the money from the checks I had given him the previous day, and that he would not have anything to buy clothes with. This is why I told Celia that I was giving her the check to pass on to him.")

Then we would go off afterwards to Santiago to change the other checks I had. On Friday night—that is, yesterday—we went to the Rivoli Theater with my girl friend, her mother, and her father. We saw *The Impostor* and the serial *La Reina Misteriosa*. We returned home and went to bed until this morning, when we were awakened at ten past seven by a knocking on the door. Señor Gamonal opened the door to a policeman, who asked him if he knew of any family called Garcés or anyone of that name. He asked me if I knew anyone of that name, and I said "No." I turned my face to the wall. First I tried to hide the checks, but the policeman had already caught sight of me. Shortly after this I was arrested.

This completed his confession, which he signed.

I V

The oddness of this "confession" struck everyone who
read it, but it struck them in different ways and they
drew different conclusions from it.

Despite the detail, it did not read like a confession of
murder at all. In the first place, Garcés never seemed to
acknowledge that his victim was dead. "I hit him—four
times—harder than I intended, and than I afterwards
wished I had," he said in effect. His whole story implied
that it never occurred to him to kill; or even that he
might possibly have done so. Yet he never said so. The
news of Mercier's murder had been splashed across the
front pages of all the popular papers, but Manuel went
on as before: the visits to the Cachás Grandes, the trips
to the cinema continued to be part of his day-to-
day routine. Nor did he ever say that though he must
have killed Mercier he never intended to. He apparently
never thought it worth saying, and though in his
confession he described in detail what he did and how
he did it he never attempted any defense of his action at
all.

On the other hand, his own stated motives made no
sense. He said he went to threaten, yet he took a
concealed weapon to Mercier's office and deliberately
kept it concealed. It was a standard arm—Chileans call
it a *chancho en bolsa*—and he used it in the standard
way: to surprise, assault, and rob. It would not in any
case have been a suitable instrument to threaten a man
with, and it was never in fact so used.

He claimed that Mercier had been deceiving him with offers of money and a job. But there had been no deceit: he had received money and given nothing in return. True, he was not to be paid for the sexual act he did perform; but he knew this in advance and was free to refuse to perform it. Besides, he had missed his appointment and arrived late without warning. The deceit, if such there had been, was the other way around.

All the same, if he had come to rob, he proceeded without much caution. In the past, when he had come to Mercier's office, the meetings had been interrupted by telephone calls or sudden visitors; yet now he appeared, unsolicited, two days late and an hour earlier than the time at which he was normally expected. He was known to his victim and was relying on a threat of blackmail to escape punishment. But he did not know how much money there was in the office, either in the safe or on Mercier himself; and so far as he knew, he took only five hundred pesos in cash.

His behavior both before and after the crime was almost equally unconcerned. He left the stone with a street vendor, went off to drink a Coca-Cola with a friend before collecting it again, and promptly appeared a day later, clad in flashy new clothes, before the vendor and showed him the watch, checks, and cash. After running away from the office, he chose to walk along the Costanera, which was known to be frequented by policemen, rather than go by bus or train or even on foot along the safer route of Calle Errázuriz. He even asked

a policeman the time. He had no fear of addressing a
policeman scarcely ten minutes after committing a
robbery, but he did not bother to examine the contents
of the wallet until over an hour later.

Even after the news of Mercier's death was common
knowledge, his routine remained unchanged. Moreover, he made no effort to hide or even to destroy
Mercier's identity cards or his casino-membership
cards. On the contrary, he kept them beside his bed,
and gratuitously displayed both watch and checkbooks
to his acquaintances. Nor did he make any serious use
of what he had gained as a result of his action. The
checks he gave away to a boy whose brother was a policeman whose normal beat was in the Cachás Grandes
area; and with the money he bought the most striking
new clothes. The haul, such as it was, he used entirely
for purposes of display.

Finally, after his arrest he not only "confessed"; he
did it in considerable detail. He seemed almost to be
laying claim to an achievement.

Hard upon his confession came a further surprise. On
the very morning that Manuel was making his statement
before the court, the owner of a small draper's shop in
Valparaíso was explaining to the police how she came to
be in possession of a forged check for fifty and a half
escudos (fifty dollars fifty), signed by Manuel with the
name "Cristián Garcés" and made out to his aunt.
(Wrongly made out, as it happened: he had used his
surname for her also.) The shop owner had known
Manuel since childhood, and the aunt was an old

customer. When Manuel appeared in the shop on the evening of May 10, asking her to cash the check, she had automatically agreed to do so, but she did not have enough money on her and had given him only twenty escudos on account. He had left the rest to pay off one of his aunt's bills, and then disappeared. So even after hearing of Mercier's death, Manuel had come in person to a shop where he had been known for years to cash a forged check under his own name. This, like the rest of the money he had stolen, he reported later in court, he had spent on "clothes, food, and trivialities." His behavior seemed completely inexplicable.

The official in charge of the investigation found the crime entirely pointless, and said so. The press reported him as having said that it was the most "absurd" he had come across in his professional life; it was rumored he had used a less polite expression. Either Manuel was exceptionally stupid—and neither his personality nor his confession suggested that he was—or he was acting with exceptional coolness and intelligence in accordance with a plan. But if he was acting in accordance with a plan, whose plan was it, and what possible object did it serve? The documents gathered in the course of the investigation suggest an answer, and the press spelled it out.

Mercier's wife and son had, of course, no knowledge of his sexual activities. He had the reputation with them of being a very reserved man who kept even his professional activities to himself, but they were confident that he had no enemies. Could it be, however, that this murder was motivated by jealousy or revenge on the part of a homosexual ring of which they had no inkling or suspicion, and not by robbery at all? Might it be that someone of legal age with a score to settle had bribed this seventeen-year-old boy to do the elderly lawyer in, knowing that the penalty for murder would fall with special lightness on a youthful scapegoat? Had Garcés fallen for the offer of a large sum of money in return for covering up for someone else?

The investigation that followed Manuel's initial declaration was designed, among other things, to test this intriguing hypothesis. It proceeded on two fronts. First, the court tried to find evidence of a homosexual ring, or at least of some man anxious to settle some score with Mercier for any reason. Mercier's friends were questioned; his personal correspondence was scrutinized, love letters from young men were followed up; Garcés was asked about his contacts.

The second line of attack consisted of an attempt to account for the discrepancies and oddnesses of Garcés' confession. He was asked questions designed to test and clarify his motives, to probe the inconsistencies of his account of how he had assaulted the lawyer and the actual condition in which the body was found, to discover if he had taken more money than he had earlier admitted he had, to find what object he had in giving away Mercier's checks to comparative strangers after signing them with his own name.

The first line of questioning led nowhere. Of course, there were plenty of people taking advantage of parties

and chance meetings in street and plaza to make initial
contacts, which they later followed up in cars or cheap
hotels or friends' apartments. Some of them knew one
another; one or two knew Mercier; the young men who
did know him told stories that in tone and substance
were very similar to the story told by Claudio Ramos. As
for Garcés, he admitted to two homosexual experiences,
both in April, prior to his relations with Mercier, but he
said that these were the only ones he had ever had. He
described his first experience in his own characteristic
style:

"In April, before Holy Week, I met a certain Patricio
in the Plaza Echaurren who pointed out to me a tall
man, well built, about thirty-five, who drove about in a
small, light-colored car, a modern one. Patricio said the
man was a homosexual and told me to ask him to give us
cigarettes. I went up to him and asked him for one. We
parted company at once; but a moment or two later he
passed in his car and invited me to get in with him. We
went along Errázuriz to the Plaza Victoria, and on the
way he told me to go to bed with him; he said he would
give me something for it. I accepted and we went off to
a place in the Banco de Crédito building. We went up
to the ninth or tenth floor. He undressed and got into
bed, wearing only a shirt and a pullover; I took off my
trousers and shoes: we had relations like that. Afterwards he gave me three escudos; three hundred pesos
extra for a sandwich and another hundred pesos for the
bus. Then he told me to forget him and not to meet him
again. I haven't seen him since, but I learned later that

he was a customs official. I never found out his name."

When subsequently confronted with a man who answered to the description and drove a small Fiat, Manuel stuck to his earlier testimony and even amplified it as follows: "I remember he told me to wash my feet next time, as they stank. And I told him to put out the light. He put it out, but turned another on; and that stayed on—it was a bluish light in a picture over the bed." Further inquiry revealed that this room was an apartment in the building owned by a friend of the customs man. He admitted there was a blue light over the bed.

The second occasion was in Viña. "I was walking down Calle Valparaíso one evening at about 7:30 p.m., looking for a pair of shoes to buy. I wanted a cheap pair, as I didn't have much money. Suddenly a Citronetta car passed by. Its driver called me over and told me to get in. He said he knew me and where I worked, which I said was not true, as I had no work. He asked me to get into the car; he wanted to have relations with me, and said he would pay me. I accepted, as I did not have enough money to buy any shoes, and we went off to Salinas beach. He put the car in a parking lot and pulled the handle of the car, and the seats tilted back like beds. Then he pulled down his trousers and I did the same, and we had relations. Afterwards he gave me three notes, which at the time I took to be three one-escudo notes, but later I spotted that one of them was for five hundred pesos. On the way back he dropped me at Caleta Abarca; he said he did not want anyone to see us, as he was well known. He did not tell me his name. As I only saw him sitting, I didn't take in his height; but he had curly hair, chestnut color, and a pale face." This man was never identified. None of this, however, added up to anything like a ring; nor could any likely enemy, indeed any enemy at all, be found to fit the bill of a man behind the scene.

The second line of questioning yielded a little new evidence. It would be well to present Garcés' further statements first, before commenting on their significance. On the subject of his motives, he had this to say: "From the very first days after meeting Mercier, I had the idea of blackmailing him, and for that purpose and in view of the fact that I used to sleep almost always on the Caleta San Mateo (a fisherman's creek near the center of the dock area), I always used to take a stone along and wrap it up in paper, thinking that on going to the lawyer's office I could threaten him with it and make him give me money, which I was very much in need of, as I had no work. But I never got the opportunity of doing so, since we used to talk a bit and then he would dismiss me from his office. I used to take the stone to his office and afterwards, when I left, I'd throw it away anywhere. This went on till the date on which I hit him. I very rarely left the stone in anyone's charge. Usually I made it look like a harmless package." So here he was saying that it *was* a *chancho en bolsa*, and yet repeating that he intended only to threaten and blackmail.

He was also to say that he "had the idea of taking checks from Mercier when Mercier wasn't looking, and

reducing them to cash," several days before he actually
stole them, and to say that he had offered them to López
even before he had taken them. So he was admitting to
an intention to rob.

The court was puzzled by the fact that Garcés
described attacking Mercier beside the sofa, whereas he
was found dying on the opposite side of the room. And
they could not make out how, on the basis of Garcés'
story, Mercier had acquired his injuries in the arms,
legs, and eyes. Garcés said he could not remember
having caused the injuries, but hazarded the idea that
"when I gagged him with his underpants I might, in the
excitement of the moment, and due to my hurry, have
handled him roughly. Due to the strength I have, I
might have made the gag too tight. I don't properly
remember." Garcés was sure, however, that when he
had hit the lawyer, he had fallen with his head onto or
at least near the sofa, and not where he was found—by
the armchair, on the opposite side of the room, near the
door. Garcés could offer no explanation of this.

The following day he had had second thoughts and
wished to "amplify and in part correct" his earlier
statements. Now he said:

"Just as I was about to go down the stairs I remembered that Mercier had told me that the door was
locked at 7:30 each evening. I remembered too that on
some occasions when I left with him he used a little key
to open the rear gate with. I also noticed he kept it in
his cardigan pocket. So I raced back to the office and got
the key—it was the only one there was on the key

ring—from his cardigan pocket. The moment I came in
I chucked the stone on the sofa and threw the overcoat
down anyhow in the room. Before I succeeded in
getting hold of the key, I heard the sound of the
elevator, and as I thought someone might be coming
into the office, I tried to move Mercier into the other
room to hide him. I took him by the arms, near the
elbows, and dragged him toward the door of the other
room. As I did so, his feet rucked up the rug and he
moaned a bit—at least I thought he did, so to make
certain, but not letting go of his arms, I kicked him
slightly on the leg and went on carrying him toward the
door. I let go of him beside the armchair, where I am
told he was found, lying on his right side. From there I
bent over him to take off his cardigan and get out the
key, but my knees knocked against his body and I lost
my balance. As I fell, I put out one hand in front of me
to protect my face, and used the other hand to hold on
to the chair, but I missed and my elbow hit Mercier in
the eye—he had his face turned up a bit. Then I took
the cardigan off him and found the key. I went out,
leaving the door open and the light on, and hurtled
down the stairs. As I was holding the key a bit apart
from the other things, I was able to put my hand in my
pocket before I reached the bottom and got it out. I had
no difficulty in opening the back gate. At that moment,
the elevator was on its way up."

This second account gives an explanation of why the
body was found on the floor by the armchair and not
beside the sofa on the other side of the room, where

Garcés claimed to have left it. It also explains why the
overcoat and scarf were found beside the body on a
rucked-up rug, and why Mercier's cardigan lay apart on
a chair, by itself. It does not of itself indicate whether
Garcés acted on his own initiative or whether he was
alone.

In answer to questions about money and checks,
Garcés now admitted that he had found more than he
had previously confessed to taking. True to himself, he
not only said he had found another fifty escudos in the
wallet; he was careful to say that he had found the bills
folded double in five notes of ten escudos each, in an
inner flap. But he did not otherwise modify his statements. He furnished a detailed account, subsequently
fully corroborated, of the checks he had given to López
and the one he had cashed himself. Luck here favored
the court. Since Garcés' arrest, in addition to the check
he had himself cashed in the draper's shop, a second
check in his handwriting and signed "Cristián Garcés"
had been questioned. It was the check presented by
López more than a week before the murder, to pay his
brother's debt for furniture, and it had been stolen at
López's own suggestion, by another sixteen-year-old
boy from the shop where he was working. Garcés had
been asked to fill it in, as his handwriting and spelling
were better, and he had simply obliged. Manuel added
that he signed it with "an imaginary name that occurred
to me, Cristián Garcés." This interesting piece of evidence clearly established that Manuel Garcés forged
checks with that name before the murder; it did not

seem at all likely therefore that his subsequent forgeries had been designed to attract attention to him. It looked more like sheer ignorance.

All this supplementary evidence came in between the fourteenth and the twenty-third of May. As early as May 16, Manuel had been asked point-blank if he had acted entirely on his own. His reply had been emphatic and unhesitating: "I must say categorically that I acted on my own. It would be very stupid of me to take the rap for someone else, who was all the time a free man walking the streets, laughing up his sleeve."

Not everyone was convinced by this, but many were. It certainly looked as if this was the work of a vain, confused boy, short of money, without imagination, and entirely ignorant of the ways of banks. It seemed most unlikely that anyone should be behind his act. Garcés himself seemed even to resent the suggestion. At any rate, by the end of May, the investigation appeared to be complete. The papers forgot about Manuel Garcés and Enrique Mercier; the entire population of Chile devoted itself to the world football matches which were to be played in its stadiums; Valparaíso and Viña prepared for the arrival of a flood of tourists, which never came; and the police were given special instructions to arrest all abandoned children found roaming the streets, as they were bad for the prestige of the country and harmful to trade. As it turned out, there were so many that the jails could not hold them and the courts in the capital restricted the arrests from fifty to ten a day.

V

Nothing appeared in the papers about Garcés in June and July. The public had in any case forgotten about him; but there was a recrudescence of interest in the first few days of August, when it leaked into the papers that Garcés had retracted his confession completely and now declared roundly and at great length that he had all along been covering up for someone else and that he had not even been present in Mercier's office when the lawyer had been murdered.

This was his new statement, made on July 30:

I am not guilty of the robbery or the murder of the lawyer Enrique Mercier. If up to now I have confessed to being, it has been to cover up for another person, who was the murderer. To make my situation clear in the investigation, I wish to say the following. Up till mid-April, I lived in the home of my mother, Rosa Herminia González; my father, Raúl Garcés Nicholson, died in 1953 and my mother married again about four years ago—a man called Angel Cabrera. Out of sheer love of adventure I left home—as I have said—in mid-April. I worked for a time loading and unloading trucks in the Cardenal Market, but I stopped on April 29. From that time on, I have been without work, and used to meet some friends in the Plaza Echaurren, who lived by stealing and robbing. During those days, perhaps a little before April 29—anyway, I was not working any longer in the market—I met a man about thirty, with a light

skin and wavy, chestnut-colored hair, in the soda fountain of the Cachás Grandes, near the Plaza Echaurren,
about midnight, who talked to me for a bit and then
asked me to have sexual relations with him. He had
hinted that he was a passive homosexual, and that he
liked very manlike men. I needed money, so I accepted
and he took me off to a hotel in Calle Bustamante (in
the dock area)—I think it was the Hotel Paris. After
having relations, he gave me two thousand pesos, and
when we left he took a bus and I went to work in the
Cardenal Market in Almendral.

I did not see this man again until May 2. I remember
the date because the day before I was invited to a *malón*
(a party to which every guest contributes with food or
drink) and couldn't go because I had no decent clothes.
At about eight in the evening, while I was by myself in
the Plaza Echaurren, I again met the stranger to whom I
have referred. He came up to talk to me and told me
that he wanted to propose a good business to me to help
me improve my financial position. I told him I should
have to look into it, as I did not want to get into trouble,
and he replied that I needn't worry, because if anything happened he would make himself responsible for
trying to help. He even said that if I was arrested he
would get me out in a few months. He also assured me
that he would give me a large sum of money at the end
of three or four months, though he did not say how
much. Later he told me to meet him again on May 4 at
about eight o'clock in the same place—that is, in the
Plaza Echaurren. I was enthusiastic about the idea of

earning a large sum of money, so I kept the appointment at the agreed time. The stranger arrived a few
minutes late, but once we were alone he asked me to
wait for him in the balcony of the Valparaíso Theater at
a particular spot, at the after-dinner show on May 7. He
was going to give me a packet containing documents.
He said he would come a little before the lights went on
at the end of the newsreel—at the start of the picture,
about ten at night. He told me that in the packet he
was going to give me there would be documents, checkbooks, a wallet, a watch, and some papers that contained the declarations I was expected to give the court
if I was arrested. He recommended that I study the
text well and if possible memorize it, and later burn it,
to leave no traces. The stranger told me that he had to
remove certain documents of interest to him, though he
did not say where from. In accordance with our agreement, I went to the after-dinner show at the Valparaíso
Theater. At about ten, the stranger came and gave me
a packet wrapped in newspaper and told me that
within two weeks he would try to get in touch with me
again. So I gave him the addresses of my mother and of
my girl friend, Judith Gamonal. Also he asked me to
read the newspapers to make the declarations contained in the documents square with the versions that
appeared in the papers. Up till that moment, he had
said nothing to connect the business with the Mercier
crime, but in the typewritten declarations that were inside the packet he alluded concretely to this man. Afterwards the stranger went off; he had asked me to leave

when the lights went on, which I did. Once outside the theater, I went to the plaza in front of the Severin Public Library and opened the packet, and saw it contained a gold watch, two checkbooks, a wallet, some visiting cards belonging to Mercier, his identity card and an entry card to the Viña Casino which was out of date, and about seven thousand pesos in notes inside the wallet. Also inside the packet were some eight typewritten sheets, foolscap, which explained the part I was supposed to have had in the robbery. The murder was not mentioned, because it was assumed that he was not going to die. The declarations contained in these papers included a wealth of detail about my supposed share in the robbery and the steps I should take after the crime. The stranger, as I have mentioned, had recommended that I dovetail these declarations with the various versions given in the newspapers the following day, asking me to modify or adapt the typewritten account according to what appeared in the news. I hid all these things beneath my shirt.

Then I went to my girl friend's house, in Forestal Alto, by bus, and arrived there about 11:30 at night. I spoke to her mother, who said that I had arrived very late. I apologized, saying that I had had some chores to do. Then I went to bed. On the following day I read the typewritten pages in the lavatory. I was told there that I had entered the office of the lawyer Mercier about seven in the evening, carrying a stone, and that at a certain moment I had taken advantage of his carelessness, while he was sitting on the sofa, and hit him on the

head with the stone. Later I was to say that I had taken
the documents and the keys from his jacket and cardigan, opened the safe with the keys, and looked for
money, but found none. I had to say that I had taken the
overcoat and scarf and fled, leaving Mercier unconscious, not dead. Then I was to say that I had gone back
to the office to put the overcoat back, and the scarf—the
things I didn't take. Then I was to say that I went down
to the first floor and opened the gate with the small key I
had taken from Mercier's cardigan pocket. Once in the
street, I was to go down Calle Prat in the direction of
Urriola to the Port Station, but not take the train. Almost
immediately afterwards I was to say that I had thrown
the keys away when I was in the Costanera. The papers
I have referred to also stated that I should say I had
taken the bus up to my mother's or my girl friend's—depending on where I was arrested. The papers also
indicated all the actions and movements I should carry
out after the crime, with all the details. They said I had
gone to the movies, to the Plaza Victoria, that I had
made visits to different places—to my mother's or girl
friend's, according to where I was actually living, and
so on. After I came out of the lavatory with the papers in
my hand, I went to buy a newspaper, and in *El
Mercurio* I learned of the Mercier crime. So I read the
declarations in the lavatory again and compared my
text with the version that appeared in the newspapers.
After I had done this, I burned the papers I had been
given and got rid of them that way. I also heard the
radio account of the crime. The instructions in the

papers also said that I should go to the Cachás Grandes and pass at least two checks from the checkbooks to anyone. I did so, and on Tuesday, May 8, I went at midday to the place where I was instructed to go and I handed two checks to Carlos López. They were totally blank; I didn't write anything on them. They were on the Banco Sud Americano. Next day I went to the Cachás Grandes again in search of López, and handed a check on the Edwards Bank to Celia Rojas. This one I did fill in myself in my own handwriting; I don't remember how much it was for. I can't remember either whether it was on the Edwards Bank or the Banco Sud Americano. On Tuesday I had gone with my girl friend to the Municipal Theater to the after-dinner show. I used to buy the papers every day. I didn't leave my girl friend's home on Thursday at all. On Friday I went with my girl friend and her mother and father to the Rivoli Theater. That was May 11. Next morning, May 12, at about seven, the police came to the house and arrested me while I was still in bed. They found me with the checkbooks, the watch, and the wallet, but I didn't have the money any more. The police then took me off to the Tercera Comisaría, where I immediately confessed to the robbery and murder of Mercier and made a statement that was fully in line with my instructions. So now I flatly deny that I am guilty of the crime of which I am accused. The truth is as I have just stated. If I accepted the responsibility for this crime, which I did not commit, it was because the stranger assured me in the second interview I had with him in the Plaza Echaurren that if anything happened to me as a result of this business he would arrange for my release after a short time. In any case, he gave me a formal promise that after three or four months he would somehow let me have five hundred escudos as a reward for my services, though he would not himself put in an appearance. The stranger also told me that if I hadn't been arrested after two weeks, he would get in touch with me anonymously to see that the five hundred escudos reached me. As I have said, the stranger never at any time specified that it was Mercier he was going to attack. He simply told me that he had to get hold of or to steal some documents, and that he needed to deflect the resulting inquiry onto someone else, which in this case was going to be me. He said that he did not want to appear to be mixed up in the matter, if the private life of the person, whom I insist he did not mention by name, should come to be investigated. The instructions about my passing checks were intended to draw attention to me when the inevitable police inquiries started up. Afterwards I found out that the stranger must have had a very intimate acquaintance with Mercier and have known him very well, because, as I said, he told me before the crime that the packet he was going to give me would contain two checkbooks, a watch, a wallet, and so on.

So I deny that I went to Mercier's office on the night of the crime; and if the elevator man and caretaker say they saw me they are not speaking the truth. I did meet Mercier in the Plaza Echaurren; I was introduced to

him about three weeks before the crime by someone
called Patricio. I don't know his surname, but he is
about eighteen. He's always in the Plaza, and lives by
stealing. I went twice to Mercier's office, which I know
because I went to varnish some furniture there. The first
time I went just to look at the furniture and the second
time to settle the price for the job; but the business itself
never came off. The first time was the day after I had
met him; the second time was the day after that. I deny
having had sexual relations with him, and I deny all
knowledge of the stone with which Mercier was killed. I
did not take it to his office. The truth is that the
declarations the stranger gave me said that he was
going to take a stone with him and leave it there, so I
had to state that I had hit Mercier with it—assuming
the newspapers said that it was the weapon used.

On the day of the crime I never left my girl friend's
house from two in the afternoon till 8:30 at night, and
then I only went out to the balcony of the Victoria
Theater to meet the stranger. My girl friend's parents
and my girl herself can prove this is true. Since the time
I have been in jail, the stranger has not got in touch with
me, but I don't consider he has double-crossed me, and
I believe he will keep his promises to me. All the same, I
have been thinking about all this a lot, and I have
decided to make the present retraction, because I am
sorry that I have got myself mixed up in a crime of
which I am innocent.

I know the name of the man whom I have referred to
as the stranger, but I don't wish to tell you what it is

for the moment, as I want to make more sure of his real identity. I have a woman friend, or acquaintance rather, who is making some inquiries for me in this respect. I shall therefore ask for another hearing in a few days' time to say quite definitely what the name of the stranger is. I think also that if I give his name now, it might frustrate the whole inquiry.

The reaction of the court to this threadbare retraction was to cite Manuel's mother; Rosa Marcelina Araya and Judith Gamonal and their parents; the elevator man; the mysterious Patricio; and the street vendor. They would also have called the caretaker, but he had died of a heart attack a month after the murder. In any event, there was no time to do more than call the street vendor and confront Manuel with him in person. For six days later, on August 4, Manuel took it all back. In a short statement, which was to be his last, he accepted full responsibility for the crime. Now indeed he went further: he explicitly confessed to the murder as such. Nothing, it seemed, was to rob him of the sole credit for his crime.

I have decided to tell you absolutely the whole truth about my part in the matters under investigation.

I and I alone am guilty of the robbery and murder of the lawyer Enrique Mercier and of the forgery of the checks that belonged to him. Very recently, since I have been detained in prison, some prisoners with whom I

Indy Opera
$55

IU opera
$90

have had frequent talks and who have experience in these things put me up to inventing a story which would justify me and show that I was not the author of the crime but only an accomplice. I was influenced by these conversations and frightened of what sentence I might get, so I asked for a hearing on July 30 in order to retract the confessions I have made since the beginning of this case, in which I admitted that I was the author of the crime. I thought it better for my defense to invent a man, whom I called the stranger, who would be the real author of the crime, and who—after he had committed it—should give me in the balcony of the Victoria Theater various things belonging to Mercier, plus the papers containing the statements that I was supposed to make to the court if I were arrested.

I invented the whole story that I told you in my retraction. The truth is that the entire thing is completely false and the product of my imagination. The day before yesterday, when you confronted me with the street vendor, who said straight out that on the evening of the crime, I had left with him the stone with which I killed Mercier, I realized that all my efforts to establish an alibi would be hopeless, as he spoke the truth. I presumed too that just as the court had confronted me with the vendor, it would have other means of showing that I was lying when I retracted my confession.

So I apologize to the court for having wasted its time, and I ratify fully all the statements I made previous to my retraction. The strict truth is that I did murder

Mercier and take his things, and that it was I who forged the checks referred to in the instrument of accusation against me.

When I told you that I would ask for another hearing to give the exact name of the stranger to whom I referred in my retraction, I did it to give myself time and to co-ordinate better the details of the story which I was thinking up. But the truth is that I did not succeed in making concrete the identity of the person on whom I was going to place all the blame for the crime. Since I have been incommunicado again for the last two days, I decided not to insist on my alibi and to come before you and tell you the strict truth about what happened, which I have just done.

This last statement received no newspaper publicity. So, when ten days later I went to the jail in search of Manuel, I did not know that once again he claimed, in court, to be the murderer.

Part 2

⊓⊔⊓⊔⊓⊔⊓⊔⊓⊔⊓⊔⊓⊔⊓⊔⊓⊔⊓⊔⊓⊔⊓⊔⊓⊔⊓⊔⊓⊔⊓⊔⊓⊔⊓

The Prisoner in Protective Custody

I sink in deep mire, where there is no standing:
I am come into deep waters, where the floods overflow me.

PSALM 69

Here the sons of adversity meet the children of calamity,
and here the children of calamity meet the offspring of sin.
Bankrupt brokers, boot-blacks and blacksmiths here assem-
ble together; and castaway tinkers, watchmakers, quill-
drivers, cobblers, doctors, farmers and lawyers compare past
experiences and talk of old times.

A man of war is a lofty, walled, and garrisoned town, like
Quebec, where the thoroughfares are mostly ramparts, and
peaceable citizens meet armed sentries at every corner. Or
it is like the lodging houses in Paris, turned upside down;
the first floor, or deck, being rented by a lord; the second, by
a select club of gentlemen; the third, by crowds of artisans;
and the fourth, by a whole rabble of common people. . . .
And with its long rows of porthole casements, a man of war
resembles a three-storey house in a suspicious part of the
town, with the basement of indefinite depth, and ugly look-
ing fellows gazing out of the windows.

Like pears closely packed, the crowded crew mutually decay
through close contact, and every plague spot is contagious.

HERMAN MELVILLE, *The White Jacket*

I

|||| The prison itself is a very large building set on
the top of one of the hills of Valparaíso, next to
the Catholic cemetery. As you approach it along a paved
road—it is only a few minutes' walk from the center of
the city—it looms up at you a little forbiddingly, a solitary, unfriendly fortress: it might be a prison anywhere
in the world. About a hundred yards from the prison
entrance, however, the paved street ends abruptly and
you find yourself walking, or rather stumbling, over
deeply rutted earth, full of small, unpredictable pot-
holes. Yet when you see the prison from the front and
on a level, its character alters; it acquires the typical appearance of a public building in Chile. It could easily be
mistaken for a hospital or a state school.

Once you are inside the main gate, this impression is
strengthened; there is a small courtyard enclosed on all
sides: by the officers' quarters, by those of the N.C.O.'s
and by a state primary school. It is all very quiet and
countrified; it seems rather like entering the grounds of
a hospital. In this section there are usually a few people
strolling around unconcernedly, looking rather like
orderlies about to leave for home, or like convalescents,
wearing the everyday clothes of poor people.

Through a door on the left you pass into the main
body of the prison, down a corridor of offices. You are
now in the cell compound. Here on my first day I
waited, in an office, to be escorted round the jail. From
this office it was easy to see the main layout of the
buildings. To my surprise, I discovered that the prison

compound itself was not at all large: in fact, though it now held over four hundred and fifty men and had taken up to six hundred, it was built to house only two hundred. It did not take up much room in the prison grounds, since it only bounded one side of a space the size of two football fields. The other three sides consisted of not very high or forbidding walls, immediately beyond which there were ordinary streets and houses. This space was indeed almost bare: the part nearest to me was a gravel football field, with two goal posts stuck at either end and a faded white Coca-Cola stand, placed conveniently near at hand. Beyond this field I could see three buildings—recreation room, printing workshop, and a shabby cookhouse with corrugated iron roofing which clattered in the wind. Alongside these, was a very solid wall dating from the colonial period, when the prison had been a Spanish fort. Beyond the barrier formed by these buildings was another, smaller area. Inside it, as I was to observe later, were a dozen or so of the officially recognized passive homosexuals, who were kept secluded from their fellow prisoners, doing the washing over open-air wooden tubs or working in the cookhouse. There were also two diminutive kitchen gardens, which belonged to two warders and were meticulously kept.

As I was waiting, the whistle blew, warning the prisoners to be back in their cells. It was five in the afternoon; in an hour it would be getting dark. The atmosphere was most unlike what I had been expecting; very casual and unhectic and human. Except for the warders, everyone was wearing his own clothes. They reminded me in some ways of factory workers reluctantly returning to work, but because of the special air of protest with which they responded to the whistle, they seemed also like stragglers from a football match or a race meeting, wending their way rather glumly home. With a staff of only one officer and some twelve N.C.O.'s responsible for discipline, a policy of easygoing concession was the only one possible. It seemed to work quite well.

The building to which they were returning with such deliberate reluctance was three-storied, built in the form of a rectangle surrounding a dark, enclosed yard. The floors were connected by a stone staircase which led up to small galleries about a meter wide, along which you moved from cell to cell. It was railed in, like a ship.

The first thing you noticed about this building was its utter decrepitude. Indescribably old and shabby and neglected, it had only eighteen cells with any glass in the windows or any electric light. The other two-hundred-odd cells had no protection at all from wind or dust or rain, nor any lighting whatever. There was no heating anywhere in the prison (not even in the officers' quarters); no system of hot water. During the roll call of the prisoners, which I attended, moving from cell to cell, I had a chance to form a general impression of their quarters. The most overpowering characteristic was stench. Acrid, pungent, and persistent, it was the smell of men who had been long unwashed. The authorities provided no soap or towels, and I saw no one use the washbasins or showers before returning to the cells.

The cells were very small—about the size of a tourist-class cabin on an ocean liner, or an English public-schoolboy's study. The only furniture provided by the prison authorities were the beds, but even this was lacking in a number of the cells. Two out of every three cells did not have a bed or a palliasse or even a blanket for each of the prisoners in them. A prisoner might have to share a narrow iron bedstead covered with a thin, dirty palliasse of straw and one threadbare army blanket with one or two of his cell mates. The sanitary arrangements in the cell, if one could dignify them by that name, consisted of a tin, used as a chamberpot; its contents were tipped from the windows into the patio beyond the compound walls used by the juveniles under eighteen. There were no basins or cupboards or pegs or shelves or ledges provided at all. Whatever else was in those cells belonged to the prisoners.

All the same, most of the cells looked far from bare or unlived in: the floors were stacked with cheap, battered suitcases, old tins, boxes, plates; tables were littered with odd foodstuffs, packets of tea, cups, spirit stove, candles; the walls plastered with pictures cut out from the popular illustrated weeklies—pin-up girls, football teams, local scenes; and there was the overpowering smell. Inside these cells you did not feel you were in a prison but in a slum. For the cells had become homes. In the case of the luckier or more privileged or more enterprising, they were also places in which to earn a living—there were toyshops, leather goods' stores, cobblers' shops, a tailor's. But such prisoners were few and far between. The vast majority of the men had no trade; no friends to bring them tools or raw materials, to act as middlemen in their relations with the outside world; the overwhelming mass did nothing, either inside or outside their cells. There was indeed nothing for them to do.

Worst off of all were the juveniles, the fifteen boys between the ages of sixteen and eighteen who lived cheek by jowl with the old offenders in four cells especially reserved for them on the ground floor. Four boys occupied each cell: by comparison with the adults' cells, they were bleak, bare, and comfortless. No glass in the windows; no spirit stove or oil lamp; the walls scratched and dirty, bare of pictures or photographs; the floors—uneven and showing puddles of dirty water—seemed of earth rather than cement. The boys had no brooms and no protection against lice. None of the cells had enough beds to go around; in one cell a boy slept on the floor. Only one of the cells had a table in it; none had chairs; one had a borrowed stove; there was one cup and one spoon for every four boys; three of the four cells had no lock and none of them was provided with any box or receptacle for the boys to keep their possessions. Each cell had a small candle, still unlit, to last the night. A tin served as chamberpot. One cell had a packet of tea. I saw nothing else.

In a prison so bare of comforts and all but devoid of the chance of employment, there was strong competi-

tion for the few cells that could boast of glass in the
windows and electric light, for the individual cells, and
for the few jobs available. To deal with this, a curious
double system of privilege had grown up. There was,
first, the official system of privileges for good conduct.
It applied necessarily to only a small minority, less than
ten per cent of the whole, but for that minority it was
very liberal. Not only did these prisoners obtain the best
accommodations available; they were also permitted to
work outside the prison, to remain outside their cells
long after the unprivileged majority had been locked in
theirs for the night, to rehearse and attend prison
concerts under the supervision of their guards, to work
in their cells at their trades—as clerks in the offices, as
orderlies to the officers, or as printers in the printing
workshop. Because all prisoners wore everyday clothes,
the privileged prisoners, who ordinarily came from the
same social class as the warders and civilian employees,
were quite indistinguishable from the prison personnel.
I was always confusing them. The master compositor in
the printing shop who showed me around and explained
his work was a discharged prisoner who had simply
kept his job in the prison—with a new, salaried status:
the only difference was that now he went home at night.
The cook in the officers' mess looked and behaved
exactly like a fat, jolly Italian chef in a small café
kitchen: actually he was in for life. After attending a
rehearsal of a concert under the supervision of a warder
in mufti, I unhesitatingly picked out a prisoner to thank

for his kind permission. I gave up trying to make any distinction in my manner to anyone.

Parallel with this system of privilege based on good conduct was an alternative, "class" system, as fully recognized as the first. The doctor guilty of abortion; the defrocked priest; the corrupt army captain; the public official caught taking bribes; the unlucky politician—these entered the prison under different auspices. They were, as it were, the scholarship boys of the system, entitled even before entry to the best positions. The candid acceptance of this prescriptive right to privilege by both the authorities and the prisoners was not, in the circumstances, at all surprising. Indeed, it was quite inevitable: the reflection inside the prison of the ordinary forms of social life outside it. In this small society you could be sure that the doctor and priest and politician all had friends or relations with contacts inside the prison administration. The "old boy" network came spontaneously into operation; the way was smoothed automatically, from the start, for the newcomer's reception. It is true that the prisoners were not permitted, in theory, to handle money; but they still owned it. And it talked no less inside the prison than outside it. In fact, inside it talked a good deal more. The middle-class professional prisoner unlucky enough to find himself behind bars possessed a power that could buy him food and command comforts and services which the administration did not in its wildest dreams think of providing. If he could afford it, he might have his meals cooked for him outside the prison and brought in daily; he was free to employ a personal valet from among the other prisoners; he could even obtain permission to build himself an apartment in the prison, if the length of his stay justified it. In one sense, these men were benefactors in the prison. They could distribute largesse and provide employment. They were its upper class.

All the privileged prisoners had a life that was markedly different in quality from that of the unprivileged majority. Two or three of them with whom I talked gave a strong impression of being so well adapted to their circumstances that they were perfectly content. The fifty-year-old cobbler whose cell was his shop, the twenty-two-year-old boy who was an orderly, the prison cook—all seemed happy men. The routines of their lives would not have been so very different outside the prison from what they were inside. They were like those prisoners of war who found that captivity seemed to agree with them. Chatty and friendly, relaxed and humorous, not only did they not behave like prisoners, they did not feel as if they were. In their conversation they always referred to the other prisoners as "they" and professed a philosophic vagueness and detachment from the life of a group which they despised and with which they felt no sort of affinity. And indeed there was none. Like shipwrecked Crusoes, they had become reconciled to their island: it had become their home. These were the kind of men who might well return to the prison after discharge, to continue with their old

jobs as civilian employees. Except for sleeping outside
the prison, their lives would otherwise be quite unchanged. A tiny enclave within the population, they
had joined "the other side." These men are the lucky
ones, the ones who have been given or have found
work; the ones who, within the prison, have achieved
what seems for them a worthwhile human life.

For the rest, however, life is very different. Awakened
at eight in the morning, after an uninterrupted fifteen-
hour spell in their cells, they are released into the prison
yard at nine. After they clean their cells, the lavatories,
and the yard, their work for the day has ceased. From
9:30 till 11:30 the adult prisoners are obliged to remain
in the cell compound, though they are free to move
from cell to cell. The juvenile offenders attend the
primary school. About eleven the administration provides the first official meal of the day: a plate of beans.
After this, until five o'clock, the prisoners are free to go
out to the football field. At four they receive their
second and last official meal: three pieces of dry bread.
They are not provided with any hot drink. Twice a
week the main meal of the day is varied: they are given
meat soup (*cazuela*). No other variation is introduced
during the year, except such as is occasioned by the
prisoner or his family. Twice a week, on Thursdays and
Sundays between two and four-thirty in the afternoon,
prisoners are allowed visitors. If none comes, the prisoner is obliged to remain in his cell. On Tuesdays and
Fridays a film is shown in the recreation room for which
he is charged. Apart from this, the prisoner may attend

Mass; play football if he has a ball, or watch if he has
not; sing, shout, stroll, stand, or sit. He may smoke, talk,
write, play games (though not cards), and read. If he
has any food of his own—brought him by relations or
bought against a voucher in the prison grocer's store—
and some sort of cooking facilities, he may cook himself
a meal or make tea. At five in the afternoon, he will
return to his cell, where he will remain locked in for
fifteen hours. The only lighting will be a candle, when
he has one; the only warmth in an entirely unprotected
cell an army blanket, which he may have to share. If he
is lucky, he will own or be able to borrow a spirit stove.
With that he may cook or brew himself some tea. This is
his daily life.

I I

In this complex, sharply stratified society there was
no doubt who were at the bottom of the social scale, the
most rightless, the least protected of the serfs: they
were the juvenile offenders, of whom Manuel Garcés
was one. How did they fare? What sort of life did they
succeed in creating for themselves? What weapons did
they have at their disposal to enable them to survive?

The answer to these questions proved surprisingly
easy to find. This was partly because a prison official,
the brother of the student who had originally invited
me, spoke to me with perfect freedom and openness
about prison conditions; partly because the boys accepted me with quite remarkable rapidity; but mainly

because the answers were taken entirely for granted by them all.

The speed and completeness with which I was accepted by the boys astonished me at the time. It was partly that I was a foreigner and thus obviously not a part of the prison system; but largely, I think, it was due to the fact that the boys' situation was so desperate that they were almost bound to respond to any offer of help. The majority of them were in for robbery, entering, petty larceny, or fraud. One was in for assault, one for vagrancy, one for rape. All were awaiting sentence; none was defended by a private lawyer; only two had ever seen the state lawyer who was in charge of their defense. At least half of them had no idea what the maximum or minimum sentences were for the offenses of which they were accused. Most had pleaded guilty. None had been in jail for less than three months; most had been in for about nine; one boy had been there for over a year, awaiting sentence on a charge of petty larceny. Two were entitled to bail, which they were unable to pay. One boy's family had never been notified that he had been arrested, and after three months he had still not found the courage to ask for paper or stamps to write to them himself.

More than half of the boys were never visited by their families, or visited so rarely that they were to all intents and purposes abandoned by them. Several boys were orphans; sometimes a boy's family—Carlos López', for instance—would refuse to visit, or even help him, out of shame. If the others were visited with any regularity,

only one received food parcels and clothes adequate to
his needs. The rest had to fend for themselves as best
they could.

In default of work, they needed something to fill the
yawning waste of their days. Papers, magazines, comics,
novels—their hunger for these was immense, it seemed
sometimes even greater than for food—and a whole
class of prisoners had arisen inside the jail to satisfy it,
by hawking old supplies, which they rented out or
traded in return for other services. The boys needed
tea, sugar, cigarettes to pass the unlit hours of the night
in their cells; and they craved the excitement, oblivion,
and sense of importance that drunkenness, sex, and
drugs afford. Indeed, they lacked almost everything.

As the weeks went by, I did what I could. It was not
much. I brought them cups and spoons; wicks for their
borrowed stoves; candles, candlesticks, whitewash,
paint, Italian tourist posters, brooms for their cells,
X-ray sheets to serve as glass for their windows, locks
and keys to guard their meager belongings, clothes and
shoes, footballs for their spare time. I saw the lawyers,
who did not come to see them, preferring to rely on
written documents to prepare their defense. I sometimes
paid their bail.

This help, which on paper may seem impressive, was
entirely inadequate to the situation, since it left un-
touched the three main problems of their life in jail: the
chronic shortage of food, the lack of work, and the
absence of any effective protection from sexual abuse or
assault. A great deal of what I did was, in any case,

wasted, due to the character and lack of organization of the boys themselves. The clothes were stolen or exchanged or sold for drugs. The cups and spoons departed as their owners were released. The broom disappeared. The locks and keys were soon mislaid. The posters all found their way into a single cell. The footballs soon wore out. The boys would break bail. Yet it did some good: the boys responded to personal help, which for a short time made a difference to their lives; and in sorting out their impossible problems in long sessions with them in a group together, I came to understand their plight and they in their turn learned to trust me.

Two boys disputed the leadership of the group. They were the same age; in every other way they could hardly have been more unlike. Poblete was a tough, the son of professional criminals, a second offender who could not imagine any other life than that of crime. He was good-looking, humorous, and cheerful, and had a good deal of personal charm; he was also disorganized, dirty, and irresponsible. He had no education worth speaking of, but he did have plenty of energy and was very popular with the adult prisoners. As a cell leader, he was frank and open, but he was merciless in his pursuit of the younger boys, and the other four rowdies gravitated around him automatically. His cell had the reputation for being the dirtiest and most disorderly of all the minors'. He had contracted syphilis in a brothel, and seemed proud of it—I overheard him tell the story, with a wealth of uproarious detail, of how he got

it—and had an illegitimate daughter. I paid his bail
shortly after I met him; he has since been trying
gradually to pay me back. As a personality, I found him,
for all his faults, immensely attractive. For him the
worst hardship of prison life was boredom.

Santos, the other boy who disputed the leadership,
was entirely different. He claimed to be the illegitimate
son of a prominent politician; he was clever, courageous,
and socially responsible; touchy, extremely authorita-
rian, vain. He was also "queer." Poblete was followed
instinctively by the toughs of the group, whose inclina-
tions he reflected; but Santos led. He organized his own
"party" both within and outside the minors' group to
fight for rights and to obtain privileges. He had work—
he did the laundry—and he used the position his job
afforded him to strengthen his hand with prisoners and
guards, and to spread his risks, which were considerable. His status among the prisoners was that of a highly
desirable woman among a pack of wolves; a dangerous
role to play. The toughs disliked but respected him.
After Poblete's departure, they toed the line. Alone of
all the boys, Santos showed some pity for the most
downtrodden boys, and at times tried even to protect
them. He was friends with Carlos López; he had no use
for Manuel Garcés; Poblete he detested. Santos did me
a number of good turns; he co-operated with me from
the start, openly allying himself with me, helping me in
every way he could. I respected and admired him.

Apart from the two leaders, there was a group of
toughs. They numbered four or five, aged sixteen or

seventeen. At most, they had had a few years' primary-school education; one of them was illiterate. They were trained for no trade; several had originally been *pelusas*—abandoned children of the slums, who slept in sewers or railway coaches, under the tables of the Cachás Grandes Café in the dock area, or in the street. They did not have much future beyond that of professional thieves. Besides this group, there were a few boys who are rather difficult to classify. One of them was Carlos López, frank, cheerful, easygoing, easily led; another was a delightful, quiet, good-looking youth of seventeen who had worked as a mechanic and had pawned a customer's radio to pay some pressing debt. He had got a girl into trouble; as a result, they had both been thrown out in the street. He now had a child. When he left prison, he had nowhere to go. Santos had invited him to stay with his mother. Another boy was an orphan, who never spoke. A fourth had parents who brought him food and clothes regularly. He was the only one who was quite well off.

At the bottom of the scale were Fuentes, Valdés, and Cantín. Fuentes had worked in a circus and been arrested three months earlier for petty theft. He was the boy whose parents had never found out where he was. He was quite lost in the prison jungle. He only spoke to me when we were alone. Valdés, who had lost his parents in the 1960 earthquake, had lived by stealing in the docks. He had been in jail for over a year, had caught syphilis in the Detention Center, and had since lost all semblance of self-respect. The third boy, Cantín, was a *pelusa* who had graduated, along with several brothers, from the Remand Home of the city, from which he had frequently run away. He came from the poorest home of the lot. He was a pathetic, hopelessly unattractive boy with a large piece of skin hanging over his ear, who set the authorities against him by his very manner. He had been raped his first night in jail.

Finally, Manuel Garcés: a big question mark.

III

The boys differed considerably among themselves in character and experience, but with one exception, they were all so poor that they faced identical problems of protection and survival. If a boy had no food, no tea, spoon, or mug, no cooking utensils or facilities, no work and no money, he could adopt the heroic course of resigning himself to the plate of beans and the three pieces of dry bread the administration provided. About half of the boys had been obliged to depend entirely on the prison authorities for the first day or so after arriving friendless and unknown; one or two of them, after discovering the alternative open to them, had attempted to live on what the regime provided. None had lasted much more than a week.

In theory they had various alternatives. They might work; they might apply for help to some prisoner whom they had known outside the jail; or they might rely on the good offices of a prisoner who might be prepared, for a consideration, to befriend them. As for the prison population at large, however, so for the boys: for the great majority, work was out of the question. Two boys had found some. Santos did laundry work, which in the eyes of prisoners and staff alike was considered as reserved for passive homosexuals; Manuel Garcés worked with a young tailor who had befriended him after his arrival, in his cell. Both therefore had cash at their disposal. Efforts had been made, and were to be made again, to give the boys something to do—breaking up boxes—but the work never lasted more than a week or two, and earned them so little that their situation was scarcely affected.

For the most part, the boys were thrown on the tender mercies of the adult prisoners, whose situation all too often was hardly better than their own. The boys who were best off were those who had been arrested as part of an adult gang. The group then continued to hang together. They pooled their joint resources and protected one another so long as they all remained in jail. These boys were normally second offenders and had some idea how to look after themselves. There were three of them. The twelve others were not so fortunate. If they were to obtain food, recreation, or protection, they had to buy them—with the only currency, in default of money, the prison recognized: sex.

There were different ways of doing this. Some men might want a boy only casually: they would offer him a meal or a few comics, a cinema ticket or some spirit alcohol in return for a single favor. One or two boys were prepared or obliged to accept such terms: they were too inexperienced or too unattractive or too notoriously degenerate to be able to command better ones. The tougher and more experienced boys, who knew the ropes, sought out those of the more well-to-do prisoners who were known to have a taste for boys, and offered themselves for cash. There was quite a brisk trade along these lines, as these men paid better and normally played the passive role. This fact left the boys, at least in their own eyes, with some shred of reputation, besides ensuring them better terms. But both these expedients were temporary stopgaps, adopted by boys who were very pressed or had no option.

As there were always plenty of men on the lookout for fresh pastures, ready to lend a boy a comic or invite him to a meal with a view to a more permanent accommodation, most boys ended by settling for a more secure arrangement in which the adult provided food, companionship, and protection in return for regular favors from the boys. The style of the invitation might vary, the terms of the relationship might be more or less relaxed, and it was always liable to breakdown. But it was about the best that boys who lacked all other aid could hope for. Some of the boys drifted easily into some such arrangement as this, either because they had been raped in their cells on arrival and had no reputation to lose, or because they imagined that the arrangement was a secret. Others needed "softening up" before they would accept it. A very few never accepted it at all.

The softening-up process was itself a part of the

traditional routine of the prison, freely spoken of by prisoners and officers alike. It was a prelude to an organized, collective rape which branded the boy who was its victim as now permanently "available." There were different gangs, each with its own well-known leader, that specialized in planning these rapes, each using a different technique. At the end of the year, when I was still working at the prison, the leader of one of the gangs was stabbed to death with his own knife by an eighteen-year-old whose cell he had entered after lockup. Normally, however, the dangers were all the other way.

As a group, the boys reproduced the features of the prison community of which they were the least privileged members. They adopted its values and copied its practices, but they were in no sense an autonomous group in their own right. They could not be: they were too poor and too defenseless to be capable of standing on their own feet as a gang, even if they had felt any sense of loyalty to one another, which they did not. Normally, each boy gravitated toward the orbit of some adult whose protection and patronage he sought; his personal interests lay more in competing with the other boys for favors than in co-operating with them toward some common objective; and the constant coming and going among the juveniles further deprived them of any *esprit de corps*.

They were, however, quite enough of a group to establish among themselves a clearly defined pecking order. Each boy's rating was soon known. The privileged were the older, tougher, and more moneyed; the privileges consisted in exploiting the boys who were younger, poorer, weaker, or more ignorant. These boys might be shoeless, hardly possess the clothes they stood up in, have no parents to visit them, own no money, and know no trade. To the older boys, they were simply the bottom of the scale. As such, they could be used automatically. The more privileged boys robbed and bullied them, they buggered them in their cells at night, they "sold" them later to the adult prisoners in return for comics or cigarettes or money for the cinema; they sent the boys to "earn" these things for them. Less commonly, they practiced extortion, demanding money, if the victim had any, or special services in return for the favor of their silence. During the day these boys became their servants—cleaning their cells, washing their cups, fetching and carrying—until their tormentors left or grew weary of them or until the victim found a strong adult protector. The boys would themselves tell me of these things when they were alone with me. They took them for granted, as a part of the order of the universe. I ended by doing so myself.

I V

Here are two stories, as told me by Santos, in his own words. They are fairly typical; I taped them both.

"When a boy first arrives at the jail, the warders take a look at him and try to size him up. If he's a quiet type, they put him in a cell with the quiet ones; if he is a noisy sort, something of a devil, they put him in with the *diablos,* the devils. Often a cell with a noisy lot will take the initiative and invite a new boy who is the same sort as themselves to share it; and if the newcomer is pleasant, fairly well-dressed and good-looking, they will do the same—even if he seems something of a 'wet,' *un débil.* In fact, the tough and the boy who has a family behind him, who will bring him food and leave him with something over to give to the others, are the only kinds of boy who are respected here. The boy with a family can be as quiet and meek and mild and unattractive as you like, but if he can give the guys some tea or sugar or buy them candles, he's safe as houses; no one will touch him. That's my situation; they are always coming around to me, buttering me up and asking for favors.

"But if a fellow is a *débil* and dirty, ill-dressed, and not at all good-looking, he'll be ignored completely. The warders will just dump him in some cell where they think he'll be all right. Well, actually, they don't really bother that much about it—they just put him wherever he happens to fit. They put Fuentes—a very quiet fellow with an Argentine accent—in a cell with the devils, for instance. There were four of them in there already: Poblete, who was the leader; Torres and Bernal, and a fellow who's left now: El Ojudo, we called him—Ox Eyes. Now, if anything is going to happen to a boy, it is always on the first or second night after his arrival here. That's when the other boys in the cell look him up and down, watch how he talks, what

sort of things he says, and then decide how to treat him.
If he talks nonsense and pretends he's a big shot, or if
he's very shy and hardly answers any of the boys'
questions, they decide he's just a *gil*. A *gil* is someone
who is dumb, ignorant, naïve, *un débil:* a fellow who
doesn't know his way around. Well, when Fuentes
arrived here, he gave the impression that he was
expecting people to be nice to him and kind and
friendly; but because he was so quiet and humble and
poor, he didn't go down at all well with people here—
even the minors didn't bother much with him.

"In his case, the boys would have made up their
minds very quickly that he was a *gil,* and they just told
him straight out what they were going to do to him.
Some boys just drop hints to start with or they begin by
propositioning a newcomer privately and promise not to
let on to the others afterwards. Others speak straight out
in front of the rest in the cell that night. If a new boy
refuses angrily and convincingly, the boys drop the
idea, but if he's polite about it, they just use a bit of
psychology and think that if he doesn't take to it the first
time, he'll give way the second, and they keep on at him
till he does. Or if they don't do that, they fool around
with him in bed and screw him that way. Sometimes
they just catch him while he's asleep. He might wake up
of course, but if he does he usually pretends not to know
what's happening. Some of the other boys in the cell
might be asleep also, but anyone interested makes a
point of staying awake and joins in afterwards. With

Fuentes they would probably just have threatened him
a bit; he would have given way at once. After all, he had
only just arrived, and he had absolutely nothing—no
tea or sugar or even bread. The bread provided by the
prison is only enough for the midday meal; there's never
anything left for the evening, and Fuentes wouldn't
have had anything to eat or smoke at night if the boys in
the cell hadn't given him tea or maté or cigarettes.

"It's not just one boy who has him; the whole lot take
part. That's the rule. They all demand their share—*la
parte del ojo*, we call it here. They usually make quite a
party of it. They start at eleven at night. Then they
make tea, light up their cigarettes, and have their
sex—sometimes in the dark, sometimes by candlelight.
They take it in turns, one after the other. At about two in
the morning, when it's all over for the night, they make
tea again and start chatting in undertones, and the
victim joins in, quite naturally. They don't usually try to
keep him out of the circle or treat him in any special
way. Well, of course, it depends a bit on what they
have done with him. If they've used his mouth, for instance, then they do separate their mugs from his or refuse to serve him or serve him last; but they only try
that with an unattractive boy.

"Next day, everyone would know what happened.
First, the minors in the other cells would be told by the
boy's own cell mates. Then the news would spread to
the adult prisoners. We call this *haciendo el cartel*,
spreading the news, or *vendiendo el muchacho*, selling

the boy. For instance, one of the minors might be having lunch in the second or third galleries with an adult prisoner, and he'd say something like this:

" 'Last night the guys in cell 47 had a fine old time.'

" 'Oh, yes?'

" 'They had one of the new boys in with them.' We say that he *dió fuego*, gave us a light—you know, when you put two cigarettes together to light one of them?

" 'Who's the boy?' the adult would ask.

" 'So-and-So'—Skinny or Fatty or whoever it was.

" 'That's good news. Where's he now?'

" 'Over there. Look, he's just going by now.'

"Then the man would say: 'Well, I must invite him up here to a meal one of these days; and if you have another go at him in the meantime, don't forget me. I'd like a look in too, you know!'

"Well, after that, it was a regular nightly business with Fuentes. He lost all sense of shame and didn't mind whether he did it in the light or in the dark. They bullied him too. He didn't have anything to sleep on when he came, and a woman from a charity organization gave him a blanket and a mattress. The other boys just took it from him.

"After a bit, Fuentes found an adult prisoner to look after him. It happened like this. When he first arrived, he used to go up to the second gallery and spend all day there with a man he met through one of the other boys. Until the boys took his mattress and blanket away from him, he used to keep them in the man's cell for safekeeping and he helped the man with odd jobs. One day another man happened to pass by the cell where Fuentes was working. He had been going from cell to cell with a bunch of old magazines under his arm, renting them out. Well, Fuentes asked if he could rent one, and the man told him he would lend him one instead. A man who wants to 'buy himself' a boy, as we say here, always starts like this—by lending him something—usually a novel. So he offered to lend Fuentes a book and invited him to come up to his cell on the third gallery to look at his collection. Of course, this man knew—or he guessed, anyway—that Fuentes had been screwed by the boys in his cell and he thought he'd do the same. Fuentes accepted his invitation, so the man asked him if he'd like to have his meals with him there and spend the day listening to his homemade radio. Knowing this man's character, I shouldn't think he'd have waited more than a day or two before popping the question to him. Another man might have come to an immediate arrangement and given him five hundred pesos [about thirty cents at that time]; some men pay as much as one escudo [then about sixty cents] for a very attractive boy. But in the case of fellows like Fuentes, the usual thing is to offer them their meals in the cell. They keep this up until the man gets fed up with the boy or they have a quarrel and the boy leaves the cell.

"After that, Fuentes spent all his time up there, lying on the man's bed, reading magazines and listening to the radio. In return, the man used to screw him every day—I know this for a fact, because I was told by the man who shared his cell, who is a great friend of mine. My friend had been invited to share Fuentes with the man, but he hadn't accepted. He told me he didn't like him much; he said he was too skinny. No, this man didn't keep him only for himself. In fact, he told me quite frankly that he had said to Fuentes: 'If someone propositions you, don't be a fool—accept. If he offers you money, take it; if he gives you clothes, take them.' And he promised to see that the boy really got what he had been promised. When Fuentes said he hadn't got any money for the movies or for cigarettes, the man himself would suggest who would want to let him 'earn' it. Of course, it was up to Fuentes whether he took that person up on it or not, but he usually did.

"Very recently, this man had a row with the minors over this boy. It happened long after the boys had lost interest in Fuentes and stopped bullying him; perhaps he had only just got around to letting the man know about their treatment of him. Anyway, the man spoke to Administration and got Fuentes transferred to another cell. I remember he said to me: 'Look, Santos,' he said, 'these bloody fools have swiped this fellow's blanket and mattress because he's dumb and can't hit back or defend himself!' He stood there, making an awful row about it in the corridor. 'All right,' I said to him, 'go ahead, defend him. That's your right; he belongs to you. But don't go shouting about it all over the place.' Of course, he's just that kind of man. You see, a man can't protect a boy from being bullied or screwed in his cell by his cell mates; and if the boy dared to complain, it would only make matters worse for him. They'd make his life hell in the prison yard and in the cell, refuse to give him anything to eat at night and make him do all the cleaning of the cells. It just wouldn't be worth it. But he can protect the boy from other men. Once a boy has acquired adult protection, the other adults lay off him.

"Of course, I don't mean it's only the boy that's been had by other boys that the men get hold of. There are plenty of boys who haven't ever been touched by minors, who are available for the men. Any boy who has his meals regularly in the second or third galleries with an adult prisoner is certain to be buggered by him: it's the price of the meal.

"In any case, up there he's always liable to sudden assault. In the first gallery there are always four warders on duty, so a boy is safe there. But in the second and third, there is only one, and he stands in the middle. From there it's very difficult to see what's going on any distance away, as you can see. So unless a boy sticks to his own floor, he's always in danger of being suddenly grabbed as he walks along the other galleries, stuck in a cell, and then assaulted by five or ten people who have been busy waiting for just this moment. If he's nice-looking and not a tough, that is. They call this a *cuelga*, a hanging. When they've got the boy in the cell, they flash a knife at him to threaten him, or they just cover his head with a blanket, put him down on a bed, and force him. When I was here for the first time two years ago, I was only fifteen and hadn't the personality I have now. There were nine boys here then; they had all been raped. There was a lot more drunkenness then, and the boys used suddenly to be seized as they walked along the ground floor and raped in the cells by two or three or half a dozen men together. At that time the worst prisoners were in the cells on the ground floor. Now they have changed them around and put the quiet and decent ones there, with the boys. But these methods are getting out of date now. Now they use drugs.

"Do you know that there are between ten and twenty people here drunk with drugs every day? Practically all the boys take them. They buy them for a hundred pesos each. They sell an old pair of shoes, or something, to get the money. They do the same to get alcohol—well, it's not alcohol exactly, it's methylated spirits from the stove, really. I take it myself in Coca-Cola; it tastes a little like brandy or cuba libre. We drink varnish also, and maté. If you take maté in lukewarm water, you can go around all day in a daze and you don't want to eat at all. Well, to get back to drugs. I took one tablet once myself to see what it was like. You become completely dizzy and you can't see properly and you feel terribly drowsy. That was after taking just one. Imagine what it must be like taking four! That's the dose most of them take. It makes them feel very happy for a short while, and then they go out like a light. That's when the adults take advantage of them. The boys don't feel a thing then. They take drugs to be in the swim and to give the impression they are grand and grown-up. They like people coming up to them and asking where they get

their supplies from. Then they say: 'You don't expect
me to tell you, do you? That's my secret; but I'll do what
I can for you.'

"Garcés takes drugs, you know. So does López. I had
a tremendous fight with López over it. Did I tell you
that I knew him before he was arrested with Garcés? I
used to meet him in the usual hangouts in the Plaza
Echaurren—the Cachás Grandes Café, La Llapa, Rock
and Roll, different bars.

"What with all the publicity in the papers after the
Mercier murder, everyone wanted to see what the two
of them looked like. López arrived in style, I can tell
you—a real Teddy boy, shouting, laughing, strutting
about, and smoking all the time. He was put in Poblete's
cell—the same as Fuentes had been. He was famous.
That night everyone envied the cell's good luck.

"During his first couple of weeks in the jail, a man
who had known him slightly outside took him up. He
had done the same with me, as a matter of fact, when I
first arrived, and helped me quite a bit. But we quarreled and I was no longer on speaking terms with him.
Well, this man started going around with López. Apart
from me, he was the only person López knew, and as
López' family were too ashamed to come and visit him,
he was dependent on this man for food. Then one day
someone asked me if I knew López. I knew what he was
getting at, so I said 'Yes: he's a young tough.' He
laughed in my face. 'What,' he said, 'anyone can have
him for the asking!' He told me there was a story going
around that López' friend had been seen lying on his

bed in the sickroom (he had been ill for a few days), stroking his face and pawing him. I had not heard it before, but I went straight off to the sickroom to see for myself. Sure enough, the two of them were together in there. I didn't say anything, just glared at them for a moment, and went out. The man had hopes all right. Apart from going around every day to watch López have a shower, he went around telling everyone he was 'softening' him up. 'Ready any time now!' he used to tell his friends. Well, López was a friend of mine, and I didn't like the sound of this at all. I decided to transfer him to my cell and keep an eye on him myself. So I went to talk to López and told him he could move into my cell, if he wanted, and I offered to give him his meals. He accepted, of course, but his friend wanted to cash in on the invitation too. In fact, the friend argued so long that he talked me into it, and I was fool enough to let him come and have his meals with us too and visit López there. Well, he brought along his odds and ends to my cell—a wardrobe, a table, some pots and spoons and things—but it didn't work out at all. He ate like a horse, for one thing, so I couldn't feed him, and for another, López went on seeing him alone. What's more, his friend had gone on spreading it about that López was being softened up. So I told him he'd have to go and I let López know that if he was so stuck on him, he could go too. I wouldn't have any more to do with him. But López didn't want to leave; so he stayed on with me.

"After that, there was big trouble. I was told that a

bunch of prisoners were preparing a *cuelga* for the boy, planning to get him up to the second or third gallery or the recreation room. There are men inside who specialize in this—a thoroughly bad lot, they are. They use knives, get out automatics, stick matches in their teeth, regular cowboy movie stuff. It makes you mad, I can tell you, when you see it. I warned López about it, but he was hopeless. You'd think I'd have been the one in danger, not he, from the way he took it. To make sure, I went off to see the leader of the gang, El Indio, and invited the gang to come to my cell to tea. For support, I asked another gang along too. They specialized in the same thing, but they were quieter. I bought some good cigarettes for the occasion, and after tea we got down to business. There were nine of us in all—four in each gang and myself. López wasn't there, of course. He didn't know anything about it, anyway.

" 'I've invited you here,' I began after tea, addressing El Indio's gang, 'to discuss something with you. I'm sure you won't object to these others being present, as they are friends of yours as well as mine, and so are neutral.'

"They said nothing, so I went on:

" 'I hear you are preparing a *cuelga* for a boy in my cell—the boy who arrived with Garcés the Mercier murderer,' I said. In this way I led into my subject.

" 'I don't even know who he is,' El Indio said. The rest of the gang agreed.

"At that moment another boy came into the cell. 'Suppose I send for López,' I said. So I called him in for a moment. After he'd left again, El Indio turned to me:

'The kid's attractive, I grant you that,' he said. 'But I've never clapped eyes on him before—much less known who he was.' I didn't realize till then that El Indio thought I was trying to keep him for myself. He began now to bargain. 'We won't touch the kid,' he said; 'but you must return us the favor.' Well, that was not what I meant at all. I was just trying to help López as a friend, that was all; and I said so to El Indio. He wouldn't have it. He stood up, turned to the others in the cell, and said: 'Well, fellows, just clear out a minute, will you? Santos and I have a bit of unfinished business to transact.' No one moved, so he got out his knife and put matches in his teeth—the old routine—trying to scare me. The leader of the other gang, who was a friend of mine, quick as a flash, got his knife out too, and they started arguing. Things began to look very nasty. I knew El Indio was very hot-tempered, quite capable of using his knife at the drop of a hat, so I tried to calm them down. 'Look,' I said, 'I was only trying to help the kid, but if you want to screw him, go ahead. I can't stop you.'

"This quietened everyone down a bit, and El Indio got ready to leave. 'Let's leave things as they are, then.'

" 'What are you going to do to the kid?' I asked him. I had to know. If they were going ahead with a *cuelga*, I'd have had to get López out of my cell. Otherwise, everyone would have thought I had been in on it. They said they weren't going to, and it was left in the air like that. It looks as if it's fizzled out, anyway."

Six weeks after I heard these stories, the tailor with whom Manuel Garcés worked was stabbed in his cell, and just after Christmas a gang leader was himself knifed and killed while attempting to rape an eighteen-year-old boy in very similar circumstances.

V

How did Manuel Garcés fit into this picture? What was his rating in the group? It was not high. I had my first inkling of this when I mentioned to the officer who was showing me around the prison that I was hoping to get to know him. The officer had expressed great surprise at my choice. There were plenty of other murderers to choose from; why pick him? False, calculating, unreliable—this was his summing up of the boy—constantly changing his story, a born poseur. He dismissed Manuel as a waste of time, and quite uninteresting.

I met Manuel on the first afternoon I visited the prison, in mid-August, when I was taken round to see the minors' cells. I was not told I was going to see him and I did not recognize him at first until he spoke. He had no idea who I was and no means of knowing that I was coming. I was in the cell only a moment or two, just long enough to ask a few routine questions, and I had great difficulty in seeing him properly because the light was fast fading and the miserable little half-candle was not yet lit. All the same, I saw enough of him on that occasion to form a definite impression of his personality.

As it happened, he was the first person I saw as I entered the cell—lying on his bunk beside the window, trying to read a comic in the half-light. The others jumped to their feet at our entry; he rose reluctantly as if he wished to make a protest against an unjustifiable intrusion. The boys were cowed and submissive in my presence and answered the questions I put to each of them in turn in quiet, scarcely audible monosyllables. Except Garcés: he replied not only for himself but also for López, and he contrived to give as full an answer as the extremely stringent limits of our conversation allowed. He even succeeded in saying they were short of cigarettes.

I did not see him again for a week. This time the boys had been given a little warning and had tried to smarten themselves up. As a result, there was considerable curiosity and some suppressed excitement as they filed into the Administration Office, which I had been lent for the occasion. I was alone now and I had an excellent view of Manuel. He came in, with López, second from last and sat down in the only place available—a bench immediately opposite my desk. He was a good deal less glamorous than his photographs had suggested. Small, dark-skinned, unkempt, with hair long and uncombed, he seemed very unlike the good-looking youth of the illustrated papers. No signs here of flashy striped pullover or modish blue jeans; just a poor boy, dressed in cheap, inadequate, grubby clothing. Nor did he strike me as particularly good-looking. Certainly, he was better built than the others and looked a good deal brighter than most of them, but if you had passed him in the street, dressed as he was then, you would not have noticed him: a poor boy, without distinctive features. His face, unsmiling, suggested he was interested, but on his guard. He was giving nothing away.

I explained that I had come to help them and told them in what way I hoped to do so—by writing up one or two of their life stories. They showed polite interest, but concentrated their attention quite naturally on their own immediate and more urgent concerns. I asked each of them in turn what he was accused of, how long he had been in jail, who his lawyer was and how often he had seen him, how often and by whom he was visited, what work he did in prison, and with whom he ate his meals. The answers to these and other questions I have already given. One or two of the boys were very shy and silent and had to be drawn out, but most gave straightforward, matter-of-fact, unblushing replies to all these questions. None tried to be funny or to impress or to show off. They made no effort to capture my attention. They were simply co-operating without fuss.

Except Manuel Garcés. His answers were, as before, not only much more detailed than those provided by the others; they were also quite different. And the tone in which they were delivered was also distinct. Again, Manuel replied on behalf of López, who was not a shy boy and could very well have replied for himself. He explained that he was accused of both murder and forgery, whereas López was charged with forgery alone. He had made just the same remarks a week earlier in his cell. This was how I recognized him. At the time, as I noted in my diary after the interview, Manuel seemed to me to be impressed by his own crime. More than this, he was very vain about it. He seemed eager to take full credit for his crime, and to be afraid only that he might be expected to share its glory with López. I was no less puzzled that he seemed to be admitting in public that he had done it, when I understood that he was proclaiming to the world that he had not.

The others complained, almost without exception, that they had no private lawyer to defend them and had not seen the lawyer provided by the state. Manuel complained that though he had both a private and a state lawyer, he had seen them "all too often." Most of the boys admitted that they were very rarely visited by anyone, but that sometimes their mother and sister came to see them. Manuel announced that he was visited regularly by his mother, sister, and girl friend.

Santos had work. He spoke of it, for obvious reasons, with some embarrassment, but he mentioned with quiet pride that he saved something to give his mother every week. Manuel boasted that he earned good money from his tailoring, that he ate well and could complain only that he did not sleep in sheets. He had much more education than the other boys and spoke better than they, but he made no effort to lead them and seemed content to bask in his own self-satisfaction. He even made a point of telling me that he did not have to attend the primary school in the morning, as his "humanistic studies" in the Commercial School rendered him exempt. So it went on: he sat there on his bench, I noted in my diary, "exuding a curious smugness and self-satisfaction." It was as if he wished to tell me that, unlike the others, he had solved the practical problems of prison life; that he was "one up" on all of them. He made no attempt to be friendly; he was out to impress.

With the boys he cut no ice at all. They did not like him, and they listened to his speeches in a kind of bored, contemptuous silence which was only interrupted when he started to speak about the tailor with whom he worked. Then Poblete could not resist suggesting, in a far from inaudible stage whisper, the interpretation the boys placed on that. Newspaper celebrity and murderer Manuel may have been; the fact gave him no sort of standing among his fellow prisoners. He talked too much; he posed; he was too "pretty." In fact, he had quite the wrong personality for the role in which the papers had cast him. As for his vaunted work and food and girl friend—particularly girl friend—these left them, to put it mildly, cold. He had been nicknamed Susie.

Two days later I met them all again. The atmosphere was now quite different. We were in a different room, for one thing—the schoolroom, which was situated in the yard beyond the cells. For another, the boys were no longer apprehensive. They trooped in, relaxed and pleased. I suggested they form a circle round my desk. After the inevitable jostling for position, who should be found seated, plumb in the middle and within inches of my table, but Garcés, with a smile of almost flirtatious

anticipation on his face. Like a bobbysoxer in front of
the current idol, he had taken the best seat to enjoy a
one-man show; he was also determined to be the section
of the audience I should best remember. He said very
little. I noticed he had two fingers missing from his right
hand, and I thawed a little toward him. At the end of
the meeting he even thanked me for some candles I had
brought for his cell—a courtesy he had omitted at the
end of the previous session, when I had given him a
packet of cigarettes. Yes, I was beginning to like him
better; but he was now angling for me.

A little over two weeks after I had first burst into
Manuel's cell, I asked to see him alone. He was not
expecting the summons and he appeared looking very
dirty, with spots of whitewash in his hair and on his
clothes, as he had been spending the day painting his
cell with the material I had brought. He was also in the
highest of spirits. For this interview I had been lent a
small dining room reserved for prison officials. It was
light and clean and reasonably free from interruption. I
was to use it for all my private interviews with Manuel
until he was transferred in October to the Detention
Center downtown. We sat side by side at the table; he
smoked. After a few preliminary remarks on my part—
I said he was free to choose any topic of conversation
he liked or start anywhere to tell me his story, if he
wished to do so—he began at once. He never had the
slightest doubt about what he wanted to do: it was to
tell me his life story, from the beginning.

Between us, however, stood the barrier of his crime.

What attitude was he going to adopt toward it? What attitude should I take up? I needed to know. It was obvious, after two or three minutes' conversation, that he did not simply *want* to tell me his story. He was burning to do so. I decided to take the bull by the horns and deal with the problem at once. Would he be prepared to speak of his crime? Certainly, he would. Would he say that he had done it or that he had not? He began at once to repeat his threadbare retraction, with small changes and additions. His whole aspect changed. "Shifty, uninventive, evasive, brief, and vague," I noted in my diary at the time; "he lied sadly, as if he knew he could not convince me. He kept his eyes away from mine." He was an exceptionally poor liar. I asked him a few questions; his story was full of holes, and I told him so. I added that an "intelligent, even clever lad" like himself would hardly have acted with such stupidity. He sat there, unhappy, defenseless. The judge had said the same, he conceded; but "it's more or less the truth." He paused a moment, thoughtful. "Let's leave the matter till we come to it," I suggested. He agreed. Without further ado, he began his story.

He spoke without any sign of nervousness and he talked without pause for an hour and a half. He spoke fast—his words came pouring out as if they could not wait to be released; he told his story systematically, in chronological order, marking by the way the places in his narrative where he would later have to go back on his tracks to give me background information about members of his family; he displayed a phenomenal

memory for small, carefully observed, and telling detail. His account of his childhood, which he began in
this session, came astonishingly alive. Though he talked
fast, in a soft-spoken, gentle voice, he did not usually
speak with much expression or feeling. Yet he behaved
like a man desperately anxious to tell everything he
knew or could remember, as if all this hoarded experience had to find expression before it was too late, and
as though this was his last chance to call attention to it
all.

I stopped him from time to time to clarify details of
dates or places or people, to ask how many brothers or
sisters he had, to get him to describe the house he lived
in, to give me the ages of the members of his family and
the names of the schools he went to. If a story made no
sense to me, because he had omitted any reference to a
possible motive, I again halted him to ask why he
thought he or someone else had acted in the way he
had. Sometimes too I found it hard to accept a story in
the form in which he told it, and raised the difficulty I
felt. He was quick to sense a problem once it was
pointed out, and made efforts to meet it by providing a
good deal more circumstantial detail, but in the matter
of motives he was usually quite unable to supply even
guesses, and when he did, he invariably supplied very
poor ones. He tolerated, but disliked, interruptions,
and if I ever digressed, he returned unerringly to the
point of departure. He was dedicated to his task from
the start, and quite determined not to be deflected.

At the end of this first session I gave him a notebook

and fountain pen to write whatever he liked and asked him to show me what he had done later. He liked the idea. I also congratulated him on the way he told me his story. It was indeed remarkable. It is now time to turn to the story he told.

Part 3

⊓⊔⊓⊔⊓⊔⊓⊔⊓⊔⊓⊔⊓⊔⊓⊔⊓⊔⊓⊔⊓⊔⊓⊔⊓⊔⊓⊔

Slum Nobody

Human life can be compared to a sentence in which different men play different parts of speech. How many people are just adjectives, interjections, conjunctions or adverbs; what a number are merely copulas; how few are nouns or verbs! KIERKEGAARD, *Journals*

I

|||| Manuel Garcés was born on October 19, 1944, in
Valparaíso. His mother earned her living, officially, by taking in washing; his father, who was about
twelve years older than she, was a traveling salesman
who specialized in jewelry. A middle-class man, he had
demeaned himself in the eyes of his family by marrying
beneath him; they never forgave his wife for the insult.
Manuel did not say—perhaps he did not know—
whether his father and mother were legally married, or
whether his father had felt obliged to marry her because
she was expecting his child. But he did say that his
father's family never allowed his mother to forget that
he had been compelled to give up another woman,
whom he loved, to live with a woman they considered
undesirable. When he died, before the age of forty, they
did not fail to accuse her of driving him by her promis-
cuity to an alcoholic's death.

Manuel was their second son; the eldest, Jaime, had
been born lame two years earlier, when his mother was
eighteen. The family lived in a nine-room adobe hut
tucked away on one of the many hills of Valparaíso,
together with his maternal grandmother and two aunts,
both of whom were married and had children of their
own. Tía Anita worked as a seamstress. Her husband
was a cattle thief who disappeared after doing a three-
year stretch in jail, and was never heard of again.
Manuel could not remember him. They had a baby
daughter two years younger than he. The other aunt,
Gloria, was married to a policeman, who also left her,

together with two small children. She worked in a bar for sailors in the dock area in town. By the time Manuel was four, his mother had given birth to another child. The number living in the house would have increased to thirteen if Manuel and his elder brother had not been sent to live with their father's unmarried sister, who occupied an apartment in a two-story house in the city, which she rented. She was more than twenty years older than his mother and implacably hostile to her. She was also relatively well-to-do. She welcomed Jaime, whom she cared for; Manuel she looked after until he was seven. Then she sent him to a poor boys' home run by nuns in the city.

Manuel did not speak much of his mother; it was evidently a subject that caused him deep embarrassment and even greater pain. His image of her had been formed by the aunt who had taken charge of him, and his memories of her were all colored by this fact. Even before his father died, when Manuel was eight, his aunt had forbidden her the house and it was only furtively that she was able to see her son at the poor boys' home to which he had been sent. After his father's death, Manuel's aunt dinned into him as an article of faith that his mother had killed his father by her adulteries and that she was now living in sin with another man. On the few occasions that Manuel saw his mother he would repeat his aunt's accusations, hoping they would be effectively denied. His mother would weep and say that they were false, but he could not believe her. Over and over again, like a hidden thread in his story, one felt the persistent, unanswered question: "Did my mother kill my father?" He kept coming back to this, and always he would answer: *"Nadie sabe"* (No one knows). All this he told me in a rapid, sad, soft-spoken, embarrassed voice, his eyes downcast, turned deliberately away from mine, his fingers fidgeting nervously before him.

His memories of his father had a different tone. His face relaxed, his eyes smiled as he spoke of him. He remembered his father playing football with him and giving him presents. This was the earliest happy memory he recorded, and he treasured it. He had not many to record. He remembered his father coming home drunk, having spent all his money; he remembered being beaten by him—but he forgave him all of this. He spoke of his father as of a distant dream: a far-off, dim, but cherished memory.

When he first moved into his aunt's house, his brother Jaime had already been living there for two years, to all intents and purposes as his aunt's child. He was fed, clothed, and housed by her; and he was looked after by her mother, his paternal grandmother, who shared the large apartment on the second floor of the house she rented. When Manuel was first brought there at the age of four, his aunt did not at once assume the same responsibility towards him as she had for his brother. She undertook to feed him, but she sent him home every evening to sleep at his parents' adobe house. This arrangement continued until he was seven, when on his aunt's initiative he was sent to his first school. He played truant from the start and it soon became obvious to this

busy woman, who had her own living to earn, that if he
was to attend school he would have to be strictly
controlled. So she sent him to a poor boys' home run by
nuns, to whom she delegated the responsibility of
looking after her nephew and seeing that he attended
class.

The poor boys' home to which Manuel was sent in
1952 is in the center of the dock area, boxed in by bars,
brothels, and mean streets and overshadowed by the
landmark of the vast La Matriz parish church. He was
not happy there. For a moment, as he was telling me
this, Manuel's vanity impelled him to pretend that it
was a fee-paying boarding school. Then he took it all
back and explained simply that it was just a home for
poor boys (*un asilo para niños de pocos recursos*),
which was virtually free. His aunt, however, who could
afford it, made a regular contribution to ensure him
more privileged treatment. (*Mi tía pagó algo a las
monjas para que me atendieran bien.*) Perhaps he was
better treated than the other boys, but from his description it sounded a pretty cheerless place. He remembered
that the fifteen or so boys who were there went frequently hungry and that they used to kill the hens the
nuns kept in the back yard and steal the eggs to
supplement their diet. The nuns used to punish them
for laziness by sticking sewing-machine needles into the
insteps of their feet. Manuel did not get on well with his
fellows. He was, on his own admission, quarrelsome,
selfish, and bossy, and always tried to make the others

play the games he wanted, while refusing to join in theirs. He was lonely and made no friends.

Before the end of his second year he was caught stealing. This incident, which Manuel recounted in great detail, took place a few days after his mother had paid one of her rare visits to the home and had given him a ball and a new blue jacket. The ball he lost almost at once in the playground of the school. It fell down a hole and his teacher, a woman, refused to let him try and rescue it. It could have been reached by a ladder, but she was too busy to attend to him properly and Manuel was too small to explain himself. He stood disconsolate and crying: he was just ignored.

Next day, when he was sweeping out her classroom, he saw a thousand-peso note on her desk. He took it and hid it in the top pocket of his new jacket. He had no idea what he was going to do with the money. He knew this was stealing—something quite different from the casual thefts of eggs, or forgetting to return small change, of which he had often been guilty in the past—but he did not know why he took the note. On the way back to the nuns' home after class, quite reckless of any possible consequences, Manuel began to spend the money. He bought some comics and oranges, which he distributed grandly to the children in the home. They expressed, he said, mild surprise at his gesture, but he told them that he had been given the money by his elder brother. They were not interested in his reasons, anyway. He had some money left over.

That night the nuns, who had been informed of the theft, discovered the telltale comics and the orange peel on the dormitory floor, and found the change in Manuel's pocket. Next day, without a word of explanation, they ordered him to pack his things. His mother and aunt appeared, grim-faced and silent, to take him home. He had been expelled.

The prelude to the theft—his angry grief at the loss of his ball—he remembered only later, after prodding from me; the theft itself and its attendant circumstances he remembered spontaneously and clearly. The sequel to his removal was seared on his memory; every moment of it remained raw and nagging in his mind. During the bus ride back to his aunt's home, the two women spoke not a single word to him. Silent, they sat side by side, staring in front of them, twin pillars of outraged pride and shame, brooding, inactive. Once inside the apartment, they led him to the kitchen range, turned the flame full on, and burned his hand. His aunt took the lead, holding him firm, not letting his hand escape the flame. His mother hovered behind her, making ineffectual efforts to help her, not daring to look. He screamed and struggled violently; his aunt remained inflexible. He remembered the blisters that rose on his hand; they lasted a week. Fury and hatred possessed him. He refused in rage to eat his supper. He was not yet nine years old.

When Manuel returned in disgrace to his aunt's home at the age of eight, the only man in the household was a rare visitor who did not live in it. He was a sort

of business partner of his aunt, a much older man, and
apparently someone of considerable means—at least in
the eyes of Manuel, who may have been exaggerating,
but whose sense of social and economic differences
seemed to me generally sharp and accurate. He was
spoken of by everyone in the house simply as The
Gentleman (El Caballero), which seems to imply that
aunt and grandmother recognized in him a man of
social status superior to their own. His infrequent but
expected visits were curiously Pasha-like and stylized in
form. He always came in the morning, rang three times
in an unmistakable manner, had a bath prepared for
him, then shaved with an imported electric razor in the
dining room, where he remained for the rest of the day,
closeted with Manuel's aunt over accounts. Though
there was no question of any sexual relations between
them, he was jealous of her and did not wish her to
marry. On set occasions, he appeared on purely social
visits and distributed gifts, money, and sweets to the
children.

On the Christmas following Manuel's removal from
the nuns' school, The Gentleman came as scheduled to
distribute gifts. He had evidently heard of the incident,
and he marked his disapproval by discriminating between Manuel and his brother in his gifts. Manuel was
offended and refused to accept his. On New Year's Eve,
El Caballero, who was reputed to be an Englishman,
appeared again and tried diplomatically to make
amends. This time he brought Manuel a much better
present than his brother: something, Manuel added

proudly, he still possessed. That evening, after his
mother had made her permitted visit, his aunt went out
with his grandmother and the two children to a nightclub near their house. It is a cheap, sordid place, right in
the brothel area of the city, but it did not seem so to
Manuel, who remembered the occasion well. For it was
here that a workman, mistaking his aunt for a maid,
danced all night with her and called round next day to
see her at her home. His aunt and grandmother laughed
patronizingly at the man's mistake, but the mistake
turned out to be theirs. Within a very short time, this
casual pickup became installed in the house. His aunt
never married the man, but she was as anxious that her
neighbors should suppose she had as she was that her
business partner should remain ignorant of his existence.
She apparently succeeded, at least for a time, in both
objects. At all events, Manuel believed that the threat of
exposing his aunt to The Gentleman would prove
potent and effective, and used it more than once.

In March of the year following his removal from
boarding school, Manuel was sent to another home for
poor boys, also run by nuns, and "Uncle" moved in to
live with his aunt. Manuel was happier at this school
than he had been at the first, for a significant reason: the
food was better and he was granted more liberty. The
boys in the home made no impression on him one way
or the other, but with the change of school that accom-
panied his entry into another home, his spirits under-
went a marked change for the better. For the first time

in his life he achieved importance. He learned to play the trumpet; he began to win prizes; he was chosen to march at the head of his class, resplendent in a diminutive drum major's uniform, and flanked on either side by two little girls, down the main streets of the city during the traditional school parades held in Chile on the twenty-first of May of each year. The fear of losing these privileges, of being stripped of his fine uniform, of being robbed of his trumpet, kept him hard at work, happy, a model pupil. (Six years later, the longing to see a photograph of himself again enjoying that brief hour of glory was to tempt him into theft and then into safebreaking.) For the time being, he had found a niche for himself, and he had no temptation to play truant.

By the time he was eleven, his aunt considered it safe to remove him from the boys' home and let him return to her own apartment. It was at this time that Manuel began the habit of roaming around the streets after school hours and ending up in the plaza, where high-school boys customarily meet to talk among themselves and eye the girls. Manuel tried to join his older brother's gang, characteristically showing off by pretending to be a high-school boy himself. He used to walk around, ostentatiously carrying his brother's texts under his arm, saying that he was a student at one of the *liceos* in the town. The gang scarcely bothered to contradict him; he was permitted, indifferently, to tag along on the fringe of the group. He saw to his chagrin that he was ignored by them and soon gave it up, blaming his lack of success

on his poor clothes. If he had friends of his own, he did
not meet them after school. The cat went walking by
himself.

He was, of course, strictly forbidden by his aunt to
roam the streets on his own, but these prohibitions were
rendered quite inoperative by his aunt's policy of
making use of him as her dun over weekends, and in the
evenings as a spy on her "husband," whom she suspected of meeting a brunette in the public parks.
Manuel welcomed this chance to escape. Anything was
better than being stuck in his aunt's apartment alone
with his grandmother; nothing seemed more inviting
than the freedom to wander round the town. The jobs
his aunt sent him on—she was far too busy or indifferent
to check his stories—gave him all the liberty he needed,
and more. By pretending that her customers were out
the first time he called, or had only given him a part of
the money they owed her, Manuel would invent occasions for "returning" to dun those he had seen already;
by claiming that he had followed his uncle about all
evening in the parks, Manuel earned valuable time to
visit the cinema, where he could normally get in free. If
he did not know one of the ushers, he usually had some
small change left over from the imaginary bus rides he
had been on, with which he could pay for his seat.
Manuel always disliked asking for a favor; he much
preferred to pay his way. He thus needed more money
than he usually had. About this time, he began to steal
his uncle's machine tools and sell them to local garages
for cash. He was never caught redhanded, but it was an

open secret in the family that he did this, and he was reprimanded by his aunt. Apart from this, however, she took no punitive measures at all—in sharp contrast to her behavior on occasions in which he was caught by an outside agency and thereby shamed the family.

While helping his uncle one day with his truck, he became involved in a serious accident. Through carelessness, his uncle backed the truck onto Manuel's right hand and broke two of his fingers. He was taken to the hospital, operated on, and cared for, but he lost the fingers. The authorities began to show what in his aunt's eyes seemed an unhealthy interest in the causes of the accident, and Manuel was required to make a statement to the police. Anxious to "make assurance double sure," his aunt bribed him with the promise of a watch, which he had long coveted, into making a declaration in his uncle's favor. The occasion remained in his memory, however, for another reason. While his aunt and he were waiting at the police station, she was approached by a well-dressed woman who took it upon herself to tell his aunt that Manuel was in need of greater care and attention than he was receiving. She accepted the woman's comments without question and bought him some pills in a pharmacy across the road. He never got the watch.

By the time he was thirteen, his relations with his aunt and uncle had settled into a pattern from which they were not to diverge. He sought the maximum freedom possible outside his aunt's home—by evading her prohibitions, by taking advantage of every loophole

in her regime, by lying and by guile. But his deepest
energies were engaged in another, even more urgent,
objective—the attempt to secure for himself a place in
the sun, to achieve status outside her house: the status
conferred by clothes. As his story developed and his
memory became even more detailed, he never failed to
describe the slightest encounter without saying what he
was wearing at the time. Usually he was ashamed of
what he wore and his standard explanation for being
snubbed or rejected by a schoolmate or a girl was the
state of his clothes; he drew a sharp line between the
clothes proper to a boy of eleven or twelve when he
wandered around his own neighborhood area shopping
and those that were *de rigueur* in the central plaza
outside school hours. He was content, in general, to
outwit his aunt's indifference through a policy of quiet
evasion; but he planned and waged campaigns to get a
new suit, or a watch; he would willingly risk a beating
to extort a new pair of shoes. And of course he remembered the smallest detail of what these things had been
like. It was an uphill struggle. His aunt must have
seemed to him all too often like the god worshipped by
the prophets of Baal: either talking or pursuing or on a
journey or sleeping. To this preoccupied divinity he
might cry aloud; but there was "neither voice nor any to
answer nor any that regarded." In default of success, he
would sneak into his brother's room, "borrow" what he
wanted for the afternoon, pack the clothes in a small
suitcase, make off with it to a nearby restaurant, and in
the lavatory exchange his own despised garments for

his brother's newer and smarter styles. He then sallied forth to make what impression he could in the plaza.

After he left primary school at the end of 1957, he moved on to a commercial school, where he was placed in the lowest class. He was now thirteen. The school was co-educational, but the classes were not and Manuel found himself in a class consisting exclusively of boys. He made friends with one boy at once, but it was a girl in a parallel class who attracted his attention and whom he wanted for a friend. She was two years older than he, and herself had a friend of her own sex, from whom she seemed inseparable. Manuel tried very hard to attract her. Every afternoon after class he went to the plaza in the hope of seeing her; he trailed after her, not daring to approach her directly or speak to her; he even followed her into cafés and hung around the jukeboxes near her on the offchance of striking up an acquaintance. In vain. She rejected him instantly and decisively: she never addressed a word to him. He soon forgot her. But she is important in his story for a number of reasons. She is the first girl to whom he responded as a person, whom he sought for herself; the first in his story even to receive the dignity of a personal name, Cecilia; and the first through whose eyes we can see Manuel independently of his vision of himself. She gave him a nickname which stuck: El Pulpo, the cadge. It hurt his feelings and he gave her up; but the name serves to give us a brief picture of the boy without money or possessions who hangs around the group asking to be given what belongs by right to others.

He started playing truant again with extreme fre-
quency, missing classes day after day. His teacher, a
woman, asked for written explanations from his aunt to
account for his absences. Manuel forged replies. His
absences became so spectacular, however, that the
teacher asked to see his aunt in person. Manuel forged a
letter explaining that his aunt was ill. Finally the
teacher went to the house to investigate, met his aunt,
and told her why she had come. Once again it appeared
that Manuel was due for expulsion.

When he returned home that day, unaware of the
storm that was brewing, he was greeted by a violence he
had not experienced since the early days when he had
been removed from the first home. His aunt beat him
severely with a belt all over—on his head, his face, his
hands, his back. She was furious and ashamed. For the
second time in his young life, he had publicly disgraced
the family. She decided he must take a job. Manuel
accepted this decision as a matter of course and went to
obtain the identity card without which it is not possible
in Chile to secure work. On the way back from the
government office to which he had applied, he met his
teacher in the street. She was a young woman, a blonde.
This was Manuel's reason for disliking her: *"las mujeres
rubias siempre me caen mal."* He told her he was going
to find work. To his surprise, she tried to dissuade him.
It then emerged that he had not been expelled; she had
not reported the matter, expecting that the mere threat
would have a sobering effect on Manuel and would be
sufficient to induce his aunt to show greater concern for

her charge. She suggested he return to school. It was an idea he found he liked.

That evening he mentioned this to his aunt. She demurred; he appealed to his uncle, who supported him. So back he went to school; but he got into deeper water a little later in the year. He was arrested by the police. Here some background explanation is necessary. The year 1958, which was the year Manuel got himself arrested, at the age of thirteen, was a very disturbed one for Chile as a whole. The country was still suffering from serious inflation; the government was weak and vacillating, without prestige or popular support; there had been serious disturbances in the two previous years. Then suddenly, without warning, transport fares were more than doubled. The reaction was immediate and violent. Buses were stoned; the police, who lost their heads, fired in the air during a demonstration and killed an unoffending student who was watching from a balcony; riots broke out; martial law was proclaimed. Unions went out on strike; as always, university students and schoolchildren followed in sympathy. There were more student demonstrations. It was during one of these that Manuel was arrested as an agitator. He and two other boys of the same age were addressing a milling crowd of schoolchildren in the main city plaza, where they normally met, when the police pounced on the three of them as ringleaders and took them off to the station for questioning. At the time, his arrest appalled him. He did not fear what the police would do to him—he was bright enough to realize that they would not do much with a throng of schoolchildren shouting outside in the street. What he feared was his aunt. What would she say when he failed to return to the apartment that evening? She was going to an evening film show, and he was due to go with her. How would she react to the discovery that he was in the hands of the police? He began to cry.

Luck favored him. He was arrested at 7:30 in the evening and released within two hours. He returned home, anxious and out of breath, a cock-and-bull story ready on his lips. But, like Madame de Guermantes before Swann, she did not wish to be late for her evening entertainment and did not trouble to inquire where he had been. It was enough that he was there on time.

His prestige with his schoolmates now rose. When the first year ended, he passed his exams. His star seemed once again to be in the ascendant.

I I

By the end of 1959, the dream of Cecilia had given place to a more solid reality in the form of a maid whom he first caught sight of behind a lace curtain as she stood at the window opposite his house, copying him picking his teeth with a toothpick. He made her acquaintance one morning at six o'clock when the two of them were on their way to buy milk. He invited her out that New Year's Day on the first date of his life. She was three years his senior; he had just turned fifteen.

Though he did not know it then, she was to be the unwitting instrument of his transformation six months later into a dangerous criminal. Now he was to spend the happiest days of his life (*los momentos más felices de mi vida*) in her company. For the first time since the death of his father he had met someone who came alive for him as a person and who promised to restore to his life its lost meaning. Manuel put this by saying that it was only after meeting her that he began to live. It was the literal truth.

The date itself was attended by a good deal of domestic drama, which Manuel remembered and described in detail. He was very anxious about its outcome, fearing he would appear ridiculous beside her. He had long discussions with his brother about it. Was he taller than she was? Was he really very small? The difference in age worried him less; it was his inexperience that disturbed him.

As it happened, their first date occurred after he had been up all night in a restaurant along the coast road, seeing the New Year in with his uncle and aunt and old grandmother. He remembered the occasion perfectly; his face softened, became wreathed in smiles. But what he remembered more vividly and described, item by item, were the clothes he himself wore to take Silvia out. Hair style, type of shirt, its color and characteristics, jacket, trousers, make of shoes; he recorded them all, detail by loving detail. He was immensely proud of himself.

The date nearly misfired from the start. When Manuel

hove into sight, Silvia gave him one long, searching look and pronounced him very "pansified" (*muy amariconado*). He was offended, but she apologized in time, and the apology mollified him. Despite this shaky beginning, the date was a great success. At last Manuel had achieved recognition. Silvia was the mirror in which his new grandeur could be seen delightfully reflected. "Lovely" (*linda*) he called her; his stock rose in the eyes of his contemporaries. As he told me this, it was evident he could still recall the flattering image of himself which he saw before him at the time. By reminding him of a moment of genuine happiness in his own life, it still had the power to touch him; but he could also smile at its absurdity. So he described, not only with remembered pleasure, but with a conscious humor without parallel in his story, how he had taken Silvia to a crowded, popular beach in Valparaíso and bought her a Coca-Cola, and how he had sat grandly beside her, looking every few minutes at the new watch he had been given as a New Year's gift that day: an additional circumstance which he felt sure gave him a new luster in the spectators' eyes.

Silvia, he admitted candidly, was also a very convenient girl friend: she did not like ices and made very few demands on his pocket. When they went out together it never cost him much more than the price of two ginger ales.

His morale was high at the beginning of this year, as his standing with both staff and pupils in the Commer-

cial School had improved sufficiently for him to be
selected by the woman teacher in charge of his class to
the coveted schoolboy posts of the year. His teacher
said he possessed initiative; among the boys and girls he
had acquired a reputation as a good dancer and speaker
and a bit of a wag. Manuel claimed for himself, in fact,
the standard qualities of a popular boy in Chile; at all
events, he was happy.

All the same, he was lucky to start his schooling at all
that year, as his aunt had other plans for him. In the
early days of February, the last month of the summer
holidays in Chile, she had put him into a turner's
workshop as an apprentice. Again he had accepted the
idea fatalistically and without much interest at the time;
his aunt had gilded the pill by telling him that in due
course she would set him up in a workshop of his own.
But the pay was very poor and he was in any case
expected to hand almost all of it over to her in return for
his keep. It left him with the equivalent of thirty cents a
week for himself: the price of two cheap seats at a
popular cinema. He was disgusted. After a couple of
weeks he gave up and refused to return. He demanded
to be sent back to school. Instead of returning to his old
school, he had wanted, apparently, to join the Escuela
de Grumetes, a sort of superior artisans' school for boys
preparatory to entry into the noncommissioned ranks of
the Chilean navy. But nothing came of this. Indeed, his
aunt was too angry with him and too ashamed even to
enroll him in the school he had been in the previous

year, and it was left to his grandmother to take the
necessary steps. His relationship with his aunt and
uncle was breaking down.

He continued to see Silvia regularly after school,
without his aunt's consent and without her official
knowledge. Outwardly, their relationship was not much
different from that of thousands of other boys and girls
of similar class and age: the standard routine of trips to
the beach, dances, small quarrels, and reconciliations.
For Manuel, it was momentous. In terms of his narrative,
apart from a brief mention of his two weeks' work in the
turner's and the perfunctory reference to school, his life
revolved round Silvia. Gradually she ceased to be a
mirror in which Manuel could admire himself and
became a person in her own right. Like Plato's released
prisoner, Manuel came to recognize that the shadows on
the walls of his cave were the signs of a willful,
independent life to whose claims some personal response was needed. In his story he begins to describe
her—what she wears, what she says, where she lives.
First it is only the hurtful things he remembers, the
words that wounded his self-esteem, the jokes that
miscarried: he seemed to remember and nurse every
humiliation. Then, slowly, a more normal picture
emerges: Silvia becomes a maid about her ordinary
business in a fairly comfortable middle-class establish-
ment—the first character in his story to appear in
recognizably human proportions. He talks in the park
with her of jobs, he dreams of independence and of

marriage. They reach, for a moment, illusory agreement.

Gradually, too, Manuel changes; a new personality can be glimpsed struggling to be born. The prisoner makes the first move to come out of his cave into the light. This comes out in his story in different ways. In his quarrels, Manuel is still his old, self-absorbed, touchy, jealous, demanding self; he still wants to shine; he does not fail to describe a dance competition in which Silvia and he won second prize—a package of cigarettes and a mug of light beer, which he did not like. He still protects himself from his aunt's interference by lying, and boasts to his brother of his social success. But in his attitudes and behavior there is a new accent. When he went out with Silvia and they disagreed, it was he who gave way; when they quarreled, he took the initiative in seeking a reconciliation. His need for her was far greater than hers for him—a fact that was obvious to Silvia, who exploited it.

"I remember that one day, about the end of March, Silvia and I had a quarrel. She said that I used to go without her to the Plaza Victoria to dance and then go on with the boys to the Avenida Perú in Viña. This wasn't so: well, of course, I did go once or twice to the Plaza, but only because I had to go to the public library there to get material or copy stuff out of the encyclopedia for school next day, that sort of thing. But she wouldn't take my word for it, so we went on quarreling. Well, about three days afterwards, one Sunday, I

decided to make it up with her. So I went and explained
that it was very silly of us to quarrel over nothing, and
said it was partly my fault and partly hers. We made up
and agreed to keep on going steady. That afternoon we
went up to her parents' house. She didn't ask me in, just
left me standing at the corner while she went in. Then
she came out again on the verandah with her brother-
in-law. He was a man of about twenty. I was waiting at
the corner, outside, quite near her house, but as her
family didn't know me, they didn't take any notice of
the fact that I was waiting there for her. From there I
could see her on the verandah, flirting openly with her
brother-in-law, holding his hand, making jokes—at least
I suppose she was, I could hear her laughing anyway.
And there was I, waiting for her outside in the road! I
waited until I caught her eye and then I made signs to
her that I was going to push off. But she signaled back
to me to hang on, and then went inside the house, I
suppose to say goodbye to her family. Anyway, she
came out again, all titivated and ready to go out, with a
handbag. But by this time I must have been waiting an
hour and a half! Imagine, in the street there, smoking
one cigarette after another! I was very angry and
refused to speak to her. We walked on together in
silence to the funicular elevator and she took my arm. I
remember there was someone else in the elevator besides us—a woman with a baby, or a man, I don't
remember now exactly; but I asked her what the devil
she was doing with her brother-in-law and what there
was between them. Was she going steady with him or

with me, I asked her. She said he was only teasing and that it meant nothing. If that was so, I said, there was no reason to allow him to take such liberties. She got annoyed at that, and told me I was making a fuss about nothing, that she could fool about with whoever she wished, that she was eighteen and was not going to take orders from anyone, certainly not from me. I had no right to tell her what she could and couldn't do. Well, by the time we had got down in the elevator, we had made up again."

So he swallowed this in silence: a new Manuel. Their relationship remained at first conventionally Platonic. This is his description of the conclusion of a Saturday evening, when he had taken her back to the house where she was employed as a maid. Her employers were out.

"I asked her to take me upstairs to have a look at the house. I just wanted to have a look at the place, that was all—I had no ulterior motive—and then push off. I was a little afraid that her employers would arrive suddenly and catch me there. As we went up the stairs, they creaked horribly; I remember I said to her that if I was ever caught up there with her, I didn't know how on earth I would get away. She just laughed and told me not to talk a lot of nonsense. This conversation sticks in my memory because I told my brother about it afterwards. He also laughed and said I showed very little tact in dealing with girls—especially ones who were older than myself and certainly had more experience. I had quite an argument with my brother over that remark. I was sure she hadn't had any dealings with men, or anything like that. Of course, I had had very few dealings with girls myself, but you could see she wasn't pushed for money, and that I was her first boy—well, if not the first, the second, anyway. We went on up. She showed me the house. Her bedroom was quite a simple one. I remember she sat at the head of her bed, while I sat at the foot, and we were talking, when suddenly we heard the sound of someone opening a door. She ran out to the balcony to look, but there was no one. I said I had better be going, as it would only lead to trouble if I was found there. So I went down the stairs and into the street. There I waited for a moment. Just as I was lighting up a cigarette, the lights of her employers' car came into sight. So I stubbed my cigarette out and started walking off, trying to look unconcerned, when the grocer's boy called across to me. He must have been in love with Silvia himself, because whenever I went into the shop to buy anything he used to say things like 'You can't go out with a girl like her—you're far too young for her,' absolutely stupid things like that. Anyway, now he called out to me: 'H'm—been seeing Silvia, have you?'

"'What's wrong with that?' I asked.

"'You'd better watch out,' he replied. 'You only just got out in time!'"

The grocer's boy was not the only one who disapproved of Manuel's courting. His aunt disliked it intensely and tried to put a stop to it by forbidding Manuel to see her. This only accentuated the tension between Manuel and his aunt. In fact, due to this friendship, Manuel's relationship with his aunt and uncle deteriorated even more rapidly than it might have been ordinarily expected to do—for a significant reason. Their treatment of him, which he had previously taken for granted, now humiliated him in front of Silvia. Things came to a head one day in the street when he was impudent to his uncle, who had found fault with the way Manuel had cleaned his taxi. A quarrel ensued which Silvia witnessed from her balcony window. This publicity enraged and humiliated Manuel, who avenged himself by striking his uncle on the head with a gasoline can. His uncle in fury beat him up in the street. There was a public scandal. Manuel, finding the weight of public opinion on his side, threatened to leave the house.

From this moment on, his relations with his aunt and uncle declined disastrously. Manuel started robbing them in earnest. One Saturday afternoon he found himself at home with nothing to do. A cousin had dropped in to see him, but they had read the papers, grown bored with their endless games of checkers, and were looking for some distraction. Their aunt was, as ever, out dunning customers; their grandmother was sitting peacefully in the living room, listening to her favorite radio program. The cousin, who was a year or two older than Manuel, suddenly had an inspiration. He pointed to a drawer in a cupboard in which his aunt kept her keys and told Manuel that it contained, among other things, an old photograph of him marching down the main streets of Valparaíso on the twenty-first of May. Wouldn't he like to look at it again? Manuel accepted the idea at once.

" 'All right,' I said, 'open it up. What else is there in the drawer, by the way?'

" 'Well,' he said, 'we aren't going to take anything besides the photograph, are we?'

" 'No, I don't think so,' I said.

" 'Because if we did, we'd only be caught,' he said.

"So he opened the drawer and pulled out a key ring from it. 'Look what I've got here. The key ring!'

"I couldn't help noticing the key to my aunt's safe among them. It was a big one, by far the largest of the bunch—solid-looking, yellow, and a very odd shape. The others were the usual small ones. In the drawer there were also some cases of lipstick: my aunt used to sell them or give them away sometimes to clients.

" 'Let's take one of these out as a present for Silvia,' I suggested.

" 'I think I'll take three and sell them,' my cousin said.

" 'We probably won't be able to sell any,' I commented. 'We don't know who to sell them to; and if we try selling them in the street, we'll only get caught. And we don't know how much to sell them for. I know what we'll do: let's take about ten of them and give them tomorrow to Silvia to sell for us. I can take them to the house and tell her they're from my aunt's shop. It'll be much easier for her to get rid of them than for us.'

"My cousin agreed. So we started looking through the

lipstick cases to find the brightest colors—the oranges and violets were the colors in most demand, according to my cousin. I didn't understand that part, myself. But he knew because he used to help my aunt sell the things and he told me that young women preferred lighter colors. The names were all written on them in American, but I didn't go by the labels myself. All this time, the key to the safe was lying on the top of the lipstick cases which we hadn't touched.

" 'Oh,' he said, 'here's the safe key. Do you know how many turns you have to give to open it?'

" 'Three,' I said.

" 'What about the key?'

" 'I don't know anything about that,' I confessed.

" 'Well, let's have a try, anyway,' he suggested, 'and while I'm at it, why don't you go and take a look at Granny? See if she's asleep.'

"I went to the dining room to see. She was listening to her favorite program on the radio—Mexican songs; she loved them. By the way, she never came out of her room to look for us; she always knew where we were. It was around three in the afternoon, and there was no chance of my aunt getting back yet. She was out collecting from a laundry.

"When I got back, my cousin handed the key to me. 'Let me know when it starts turning in the lock,' he said.

"As luck would have it, it started turning right away. I don't know even now how I did it, but I got it just right the first time, and the safe opened right away.

" 'How much is there inside?' he asked.

" 'We'd better not take too much,' I cautioned, 'or Tía Berta will notice. If we are likely to get caught, I'd rather not take anything.'

"I don't remember now what I thought might happen, but I was definitely scared of being found out.

" 'No, she won't catch us.'

"We started taking out the money. We were just counting it when I heard Granny calling to us. The first thing I did was to say 'Put it all back!—she mustn't cotton on to what we're up to!' and I began to sweat. I always do when I'm nervous. Then I went along the passage to where Granny was. 'What's going on? Where are you two?' she asked me.

" 'We're playing checkers,' I told her. She asked me to let her know when Tía Berta got in. That wouldn't be for at least half an hour.

"Then I returned to my cousin. 'Let's get on with it,' he said. And we did."

Manuel took a thousand pesos (at that time, slightly over a dollar) from the safe. The two boys had to sell the lipstick themselves, as Silvia said she was too busy to do it for them. Their aunt missed nothing. Four days later, however, emboldened by their success, they opened the safe again. There was still plenty of money there. The cousin took twenty thousand pesos, which he spent on a trip to the capital; Manuel, who took only five thousand, spent his on a birthday present for his aunt! Shortly afterwards, his aunt discovered the loss. She was most suspicious of the other boy and accused him first. He denied everything. Then she turned on Manuel. He accused his uncle. It was a possible tactic, and it worked. His aunt said nothing to his uncle, but she hid the keys.

Manuel's relations with his uncle were even worse. He was expected to work for him, keeping his taxi clean, but they were on bad terms, made worse by Manuel's objection to the way his uncle would manhandle and punch him while pretending humor. One morning, on impulse, after a quarrel with his uncle, Manuel opened the toolbox in the back of the car, removed a jack, and sold it to a nearby garage. His uncle noticed its disappearance and at once suspected who the thief was. That afternoon his uncle and aunt drove him off in the taxi to the Oficina de Investigaciones, where his aunt had a contact. Manuel was marched in front of a desk and subjected to a cross-examination about the missing tool. He denied all knowledge of it. He was then taken and shown a door where, he was told, he would have electric currents applied to him and ammonia put up his nose if he delayed his confession much longer. Intimidated, he confessed. Mollified by this collapse, his uncle and aunt then took him home again.

Things reached a climax a few days later. He had gone out, as usual on a Saturday night, with Silvia, and had returned with her to the kitchen of the house in which she worked, when her employers unexpectedly returned. She was not permitted to have callers, so she hid him in her room. Manuel was trapped. There was nothing but to stay the night. "First, I undressed and got into bed. Then she did. We had sexual relations. It was the first time in my life." He was fifteen.

Next morning at six-thirty he dressed and with his shoes in his hands crept down the creaking stairs. So alarmed was he that he did not dare put on his shoes till he was safely out in the street, where he was seen by the grocer's boy in the shop next door. The boy was quick to put two and two together and could not resist making a crack. Manuel was not amused. His next problem was to get back into his own house. He had no key and had to get the milk before the family got up. He was obliged to ring.

By the time he had returned with the milk and breakfast had been prepared, he realized he was in for big trouble. His uncle took no part in it, remaining in bed throughout the ensuing scene; but his aunt and his brother, who were certain that he had spent the night with Silvia, felt that this time he had gone too far. He was ordered out of the house. He never went back.

He packed a couple of suitcases, left them with the proprietor of a shop, and spent the day wandering the streets. He bought a newspaper, ate in soda fountains, went that evening to see Silvia. He said nothing about being turned out of his aunt's home. He spent the night with Silvia again—this time at her express invitation.

By Monday, however, Manuel had had time to take stock of his situation and he decided to move into a hotel owned by a woman who was an old client of his aunt's and had taken his side against his aunt in his quarrels with her. It was characteristic of Manuel's experience of older women—other than his mother and his aunt—that they spontaneously offered him help. So in this instance: when he registered, she refused his money, which he had been given as a farewell present by his grandmother. She let him stay at the hotel for four days free. It did not occur to Manuel to return to his mother's home or eat there, or even to let her know that he had left his aunt's, until his money ran out. Nor did his mother, who had been independently informed of his departure, make any move toward him. Meanwhile, Manuel thought vaguely of trying to get a job; he spent the next few days wandering around the streets, eating sandwiches in milk bars. A new routine of life was beginning.

In the evening he went to see Silvia again. He was surprised to be told that she was away and had left no message. He called again the following day: she had not returned. He went to her parents' home; he was received with hostility. Silvia had left word that she would have nothing more to do with him. He could not believe his ears. A day or two later—he had been hanging around in the hope of seeing her—he caught sight of her as she was about to return home in the lift up the hill. He joined her; she sent him packing. He had cost her her job.

After four days, his money spent, he returned to his mother's adobe home. She welcomed him back and reproached him for not coming sooner. Manuel's comment on his homecoming was that his mother did not make any mention of his need to find a job, and that he

made no move to look for one. There had been, inevi-
tably, considerable changes in the household since he
had left it more than ten years earlier. To start with, it
was not the same house. The family had moved into
another adobe house on another hill. His mother had
also married again—this time a lineman on the railroad
who worked outside Valparaíso and returned home
only rarely and for short visits. His maternal grandmother was still living with his mother; his mother had
two more children by her second husband, Manuel's
stepfather. Tía Anita's husband had left her many years
before, but she now had a thirteen-year-old daughter to
bring up and still worked as a seamstress in a Valparaíso
factory downtown. Tía Gloria, on the other hand, had
made good. She had long ago got rid of her policeman
husband and was now running a bar of her own in the
dock area. In addition, she now had three children of
her own. It was to this house that Manuel returned in
May 1960, to share a bedroom with his cousin Pablo,
Tía Gloria's son. They were the same age and hit it off
quite well. Sometimes they went out in the evenings
together after Pablo had finished his work.

Manuel could not get Silvia out of his mind, however,
and went in search of her again. This time he tracked
her down to a glass shop where she had found work.
But she was adamant; she would have nothing to do
with him. Deeply upset by this rejection—*amargado*
was Manuel's own word—he went off to a café and
drank beer after beer till he was completely drunk.
Standing dizzy and helpless in the street, he was

recognized by a taxi driver who knew his uncle, and driven home. It was his first experience of complete intoxication: he was not yet sixteen. His mother, he said, must have hit him hard when he arrived, because the following morning, on examining himself in the mirror at home, he was surprised to see a large black eye. Certainly, she was very angry with him and demanded that he find a job. So he went out to buy a paper and scan the help wanted columns. Seeing several appropriate offers, he chose the one nearest the place where Silvia worked and set out to apply for the position. He was taken on at once as bellboy in a cheap boarding-house. The wages were reasonable (he remembered exactly how much they had been), and the house had the advantage, as he remarked, of being within striking distance of the shop where Silvia worked.

If, however, he hoped that time would help to renew his friendship with her, he was to be bitterly disappointed. Within two weeks, he saw her in the street in the arms of a sailor. He stood watching; he even waited for the sailor to kiss her goodbye and walk past him. Manuel was so upset that he returned home at once and decided to give up his job. His mother, however, would not hear of it and the moment passed. He lingered on a short while longer, but the job no longer had a *raison d'être*. Before the month was out, he had quarreled with his boss on a matter of pride—whether he should clean the residents' shoes—and quit. For two years he was not to hold a job for so long again.

With the loss of all hope in Silvia, Manuel's life now

darkened. He made no further effort to get a job. He
returned to the haunts of his schooldays—the central
plaza, dominated by the cathedral, the plaza of all his
secret triumphs and defeats; he joined a gang, whose
leaders specialized in peddling marijuana. At first his
role was a minor one. He was, after all, much younger
than the other members, whose ages ranged from
eighteen to twenty-one. As the new boy, they employed
him as messenger between buyer and seller. His func-
tion was to take a sealed envelope from one man whom
he did not know to another in the neighboring town of
Viña. He did not know what the envelope contained,
but he was paid weekly nearly three times what he had
earned as bellboy in the boardinghouse. The job was
dangerous and he knew it.

Before long, his contact man was nabbed by the
police, and Manuel found himself unexpectedly in
possession of an envelope he was unable to deliver. He
opened it. Inside, he found four hundred thousand
pesos in notes—an unheard of windfall; the price of a
new motorcycle. Manuel did not hesitate. Selecting two
toughs he knew in the gang, he gave them ten thousand
pesos each in return for their protection and willingness
to back up his story that he had never been given an
envelope, should his contact be inconveniently released
by the police. The precaution proved necessary. Within
two days his contact did appear again to claim his prize.
Of course he did not believe Manuel, but the plan
worked like clockwork. The toughs appeared as if from

nowhere and backed Manuel up. Manuel had won the first round.

Manuel's method of handling the money he had stolen included no attempt at concealment and betrayed no regard for consequences. Though he protected himself within limits by providing himself with a set of false papers, and by taking the name of a boy who had been at school with him—Christián Nicholls, who had been widely regarded as his spit image—he at once spent the bulk of what represented a considerable fortune on buying a Vespa. The notary before whom he was required to make a sworn declaration to have the sale authorized was suspicious of the source of his wealth, asked him some searching questions, but then lost all interest. Manuel's forged papers established his age as over eighteen; the driving test proved no obstacle. He was given his licence.

His standing with the gang rose and his participation in their activities accordingly increased. They extended their range of action and began a campaign of violence along the seafront of Viña at night, which lasted for some weeks and succeeded in hitting the headlines of the local papers. They followed Vespa drivers and attacked them, throwing their machines into the sea; they set on young lovers as they walked arm in arm in the public parks. They broke street lights and smashed glass. Manuel went one better. He staged an armed holdup. With a confederate, he drove to a crowded café at midnight. The other boy entered, held up the cashier

with a toy pistol, took the cash, and sped off into the
night with Manuel, who was waiting on his new scooter
outside. As Manuel told me this, he added, with quiet
but unmistakable satisfaction, that their exploits had got
into the papers—"without the names, of course." The
boys were never caught.

The police, however, had their eye on the gang. The
constant arrests of the marijuana contact men and the
success with which the authorities shortly after put a
stop to the whole trade make this clear. They also tried
to infiltrate the group by introducing young detectives
into the gang in the guise of gang members. One such
detective was murdered for his pains. He had been
mingling with the boys, apparently successfully, in the
plaza, and collecting information; then someone became
suspicious. He was asking, to start with, far too many
questions—a clear infringement of the gang code. The
group took action at once. Corraling him in the plaza,
they moved as a group, with the unfortunate detective a
virtual prisoner in their midst, to a relatively deserted
side street barely fifty yards from the cathedral. There
they set upon him with such ferocity that they killed
him. Manuel was careful to say that he himself had not
been present at this act of revenge, but his absence was
accidental and he clearly showed the attitude of the
gang toward the killing. The detective was, after all, a
representative of the gang's Public Enemy Number
One—indeed, a member, in the boys' eyes, of the
biggest and most dangerous gang of all, the police.
Manuel made this point explicitly. Had I seen, he asked

me, the short paragraphs that appeared in the back pages of the papers, announcing in small, unemphatic print that a man had been found dead in the street, without papers or any means of identification? Those were the men, Manuel asserted, that the police had arrested on suspicion, beaten up, and then left for dead in the streets. It was the special contribution of Investigaciones to the perfect crime. The gang was only hitting back, breaking the weakest link in the long police chain. This young detective had bungled his job: he deserved what he got. It was as simple as that.

It was, however, typical of Manuel's confusion of mind that, having told me of this murder, he should add that the gang only meant to beat up the detective and teach him a lesson: as if they would dare to risk police reprisals. Five of the boys were run in for questioning, Manuel included. They were released for lack of evidence.

Due partly to Manuel's growing prestige in the group and partly to his intelligence and coolness, he graduated into being a contact man himself. His new job was to buy the marijuana direct from the man in the Viña Plaza and sell it direct to customers in the Central Plaza in Valparaíso. His cleverness was his undoing. He undersold his competitors, and the man with whom he traded was arrested and sentenced. Manuel was suspected of having given him away.

Driving back from Viña one night along the coast road, Manuel found himself under attack by six muffled, goggled figures on Vespas. He was badly beaten up.

It was now his turn to see his Vespa smashed gratuitously and hurled over the rocks into the sea. He did
not know at the time who had done this to him, but
a week later, in case he had failed to read the writing on
the wall, its message was clearly spelled out to him. The
men came and warned him in person: keep out of the
marijuana business. He took their advice. He had now
spent all his money and lost his Vespa to boot.

I asked him what he did with the money he had made
in the business and from his holdup. The sums he
mentioned seemed respectable. He looked blank and
vague; he really did not know. "Just spent it on food,
cigarettes, clothes—that sort of thing," he said. Probably
he spent a good deal of it showing off to the gang. He
never gave his mother anything toward his keep; nor
did she ask where he was working, or how he earned his
money, or how much. She was even satisfied that the
Vespa was on permanent loan from a friend. He rarely
ate, smoking incessantly instead—this staved off hunger and took away appetite. When he needed food, he
ate a sandwich at a café at night. He did not himself
smoke marijuana.

By the end of the year, after being beaten up, he
returned to "honest" work. Recommended by a friend,
he went to work in the kitchen of a boardinghouse. He
continued to use his forged papers and he lasted there
no longer than he had in his first job. Within a month he
had again walked out—this time with eighty thousand
pesos; money he had found in an envelope he was given
to take to the butcher's. He took it because the opportu-

nity presented itself. He had no idea whatever what he was going to do with it. He junked the bicycle he was riding at the time, and when he returned home and saw the police van waiting outside his house to arrest him, he went into hiding with a friend.

His demoralization was by now complete. A girl friend of the boy with whom he was staying saw him one day and was evidently attracted by him, for she took the trouble to meet him and invite him to her home. Her name was Susana, and she had a car—or rather her parents, who were away in the capital, had left their Buick in the garage. She asked Manuel if he could drive it. On his mettle, he said he could, so she invited him to drive her and some friends to a party which was being given by some students in a country town some thirty miles outside the city. Manuel was apprehensive. He had no right to drive a car, as he was under age, and though he possessed forged papers he was not anxious to expose himself to trouble. Besides, I suspect that he did not want to go: Susana and her friends were not his class. But she taunted him with cowardice, and he accepted out of pride. When they arrived at the country boardinghouse, it was overrun with teen-age students, dancing and "whooping it up." After the party, they stayed the night in the place. Manuel retired to his bed alone, but Susana had other ideas. She entered his room when he was already in bed and slipped in beside him. "This was the third time I had relations with a girl." He woke up late, to the sound of knocking on his door. He was embarrassed and shouted that he wanted no breakfast. The knocking was a practical joke. It was only one of the boys who had come to ask if Susana was in bed with him. He replied simply "Yes."

When Manuel first told me this story, he glamorized it. He played up the difficulties of his undertaking—his youth, his lack of proper documents, the gauntlet of police he had to run on the way there and back, his general insouciance. He described a visit to a house where he had obtained false papers. The whole story had the false, contrived air of a film sequence. Even so, one could see that it had not been a success. When I returned to this story some six weeks later, most of the glamour had dropped off. The forged papers he already possessed: he never thought of them particularly at the time. He had been signaled to stop twice, not "fifteen times," as he had said earlier. The party sounded very ordinary on second telling. He admitted also, when pressed on the point, that he had not enjoyed himself. The boys and girls who were there he did not know; they were noticeably better educated and better dressed than he, and by their manner toward him made him feel inferior. Even the treatment accorded to him by Susana offended him: she seemed to be secretly sneering at his conversation. He reacted by pretending that the car belonged to his father, who was a millionaire. The boys countered by pointing to his cheap, inferior clothes. He said they were the fashion: he was wearing dirty blue jeans deliberately. His "night of love" was not much of a success either. Perhaps Susana only served to remind him of the lost Silvia. The following day he went to see Susana; he wanted to break off with her and her group. She tried to dissuade him. So he gave her a vague and reluctant promise to see her again soon. He never did.

With the approach of Christmas, he returned home and prepared for a succession of casual parties in cafés, bars, and working-class clubhouses to celebrate the season in style. He wandered off to see a woman who kept a snack bar and have a Christmas Eve dinner with her and her husband. He had met them casually during the year, when he had worked for a couple of days in a pastry cook's. He stayed with them until midnight, when his cousin and a friend of his joined him and the party broke up for the night. He met a girl who had served drinks, as they left the soda fountain together, and offered to see her home. He thought of attending Midnight Mass, but the idea then slipped his mind. He was rather drunk. After seeing Gaby, the girl, home in a taxi, his cousin, his friend, and Manuel wandered off to a clubhouse where there was dancing. Manuel was sick. He fell asleep at a table and woke up in the early hours to see the table littered with empty wineglasses and a half-eaten sandwich still in his hand. The three of them left, but got no further than the main plaza. Drugged with spirits and wine and sleep, they all collapsed on a bench. They were awakened at nine by a policeman. They were surprised that no one had robbed them.

The days that followed Christmas 1960 passed in much the same way. Now that Manuel had exhausted his money, it looked as if his holiday was at an end. As luck would have it, however, he went in search of his cousin Pablo, who was working at a fruit store, and while waiting for him upstairs in a hairdressing salon also kept by his cousin's employer, Manuel saw a cutthroat razor, which he pocketed without further reflection. He sold it in the market. It would keep the wolf from the door for a short time anyway. Then he went off in search of the gang.

The rest of Manuel's story, which follows continuously from this point, is told in the first person. It was recorded after he had been transferred from the prison to the Detention Center downtown.

Part 4

"I and I Alone"

Call me Ishmael.   HERMAN MELVILLE, *Moby Dick*

|||| The gang were all about seventeen or so. I was
        the youngest—all fellows who had no use for
their homes, just bored there; we had no interest in our
families, none at all. My mother was never interested in
me either. All she ever wanted to know was whether I
was working. I invited the boys to go dancing in the
Pérgola de Italia: a few girls tagged along with us as
well, but I got bored and drifted back to the Plaza.
There I played crap with some other guys till about five
in the morning, when a cop came and we had to take
cover in Bellavista Station. By the time it was morning,
we got fed up with this—I had won a little, by the way:
about four escudos—and tried to think of some other
entertainment. The losers went off home, but the rest of
us bought a paper and looked to see what was on at the
races. They looked interesting, so we pushed off there
for the morning, and I was lucky again, and won another four and a half escudos. The afternoon I spent in
the movie beside the Plaza Victoria. I joined the gang
again afterwards and we went dancing in the Pérgola,
as we had the previous night. I had quite a bit of money,
of course, but as the party was on me, it soon went up in
smoke. Back in the Plaza, we were wondering how to
get hold of some more—who would lend us some or
what we could pawn—when I saw my cousin marching
along with a hefty fellow whom I knew slightly. I
thought to myself, "He's come about the razor," and
tried to make myself scarce. My idea was to get lost in
the crowd in the small plaza in front of the Public Library, and I crossed the road; unfortunately, my cousin

spotted me and started to run after me. So I slipped
down a side street and hid inside a doorway, making
sure to shut the door which led into the street. While I
was hiding there, I could hear their footsteps getting
nearer and their voices as they shouted to each other:
"He's gone down there," or "No, let's go this way," and
so on. Then I heard them say: "Look, this is the only
door closed; he must be in there!" And they rang the
doorbell. Well, when the lady of the house opened her
door and saw me cowering there in the porch, she cried
out: "What are you doing there, young fellow?" I replied: "Please don't give me away, señora; those two
outside are after me." But she called her husband,
opened the door, and pushed me out. My cousin
grabbed me and wouldn't let me go. The two of them
took me off to the fruit store belonging to the señora,
where Pablo worked. On the way I remember we passed
some friends and the boys told me to pretend I was
just drunk and they were helping me home. When we
got to the señora, she said: "Well, where is that razor?"
"I don't know," I said. "You stole it," she said, accus-
ingly. Then I admitted I had taken it and began to cry,
and her husband started bawling me out. Meanwhile,
Pablo had gone off to fetch my mother. When she
arrived, the señora told her that she was going to have
me arrested. My *mamá* did not raise any objection; she
just turned to me and said: "Manolito, why do you
have to go around stealing things?" "*Mamá*," I said, "I
only took it because I don't have a razor. Now I've sold
it." I asked the señora if I couldn't give her the money

to buy a new one, but she refused. "No, I am going to take you to the police station. That will teach you not to steal." My cousin and the other fellow took me between them, my mother and the señora followed in the rear. No one spoke. It was about eleven or twelve at night.

At the station we were kept waiting quite a long time, and I began to smoke. I felt very nervous, as I didn't know what was in store for me. They took my belt and shoelaces and put me in a cell marked "Minors." It was pitch dark in there—I couldn't see a thing at first—and it had no windows: there was only a little peephole for the warder to look through. It smelt horrible, and there were quite a lot of small boys in there. Some of them were still awake. I remember one boy in particular—he was only ten—who called me *Corril* (Chief) and asked me for a cigarette. When I lit a match for him, I saw his face—he was a *pelusa*, a deserted slum child, very dirty he was. The boys treated me very respectfully, as if I were grown up.

I couldn't sleep at all that night. I didn't lie down or even sit in the cell, I just kept pacing up and down. I couldn't even lean against the walls. Whenever I put my hands against them I felt something sticky, and I had to walk about in the cell very gingerly too, as the boys were lying on the floor. When it began to get light, I had a look at the cell. The walls were painted with fresh tar halfway up. Above that there was dirty whitewash, covered with scrawls: "Juanito was here"—things like that. In the corner was a lavatory—elephant's feet type: completely filthy, stuffed with dirty paper and dry excrement. The floor was of cement, but there were a few boards on the ground, and there the six or seven boys in the cell were sleeping, in a *carril*, a semicircle, their bodies all tightly packed together, one against the other to keep warm. The rest of the floor was covered with filth and was crawling with lice and bugs that breed in wood. The boys were nearly all very poorly dressed, and without shoes. Practically all very young —four, five, and seven years old, mostly; *pelusas*. Only one of them was a little older. He was about fifteen—a year younger than I; he asked me why I was there. He was better dressed and spoke better than the others; you could see he wasn't a *pelusa*. Well, I told him all about the razor business. "That's larceny," he said. I don't understand how he knew the legal names, but I suppose he had been a thief before. He was called Sebastián; he was in for fraud.

In the morning they let all the *pelusas* out; they were just there for the night. Of course, they didn't give any of us breakfast or anything to drink. When they came to give us back our things, I only got back one of the two packs of cigarettes I had, and complained; but I got back my money, wristwatch, and ring. Then they took Sebastián and me off in a police van to Investigaciones. On the way, Sebastián kept saying to me: "Deny everything; they'll beat you up, but it's better to put up with that than have to spend about eighteen months in jail." "All right," I said, "I will." Well, the joke was that Investigaciones were after him, not me. I was just brought here—to the Detention Center—along with a

lot of drunks who had been picked up at Investigaciones
when we stopped there. At about seven we were all
dumped in a small yard here to wait to be allocated
cells. It was New Year's Eve; I was feeling very depressed. I even thought of trying to escape. Afterwards
I forgot about it. Everyone kept telling me I should be
out soon anyway, and it would be silly to try and run
away.

While we were waiting, a gentleman—well, he was
just a drunk, really—said to me: "You'd better try to
collect some papers to sleep on, young fellow; they
won't give you anything here." "I am sure my *mamá* will
bring me some blankets," I told him. "They don't allow
anyone to bring anything in here," he said, "and the
cells are awful, I can tell you." (He thought I was
another of the drunks, as I had been put with them).
Then they made us all get in line to take down our
particulars.

"What are you here for?" they asked me. "I took a
razor," I started, and then went on to tell them the
whole story—how I had gone to the market and sold it,
all that stuff. Of course, I wouldn't do that now: for
instance, the last time I was brought in here I didn't
explain anything. When they asked me, I just said
shortly: "Murder." Then it was different: I didn't know.
"Larceny, then," the sergeant said when he heard my
story. "We'll put you in 'Juveniles.' "

I was shown where to sleep and given a couple of
blankets. It was a cell for twelve, with bunks in it; I had
one of the bottom ones. Some of the fellows who were in

there looked me up and down and then told me to go
and collect the milk. I didn't want to go; I thought they
were pulling my leg, but the corporal in charge also told
me to go, so I was reassured. I was given a voucher to
take to the kitchen. But when I got there I was told it
was made out wrong. "It says only ten liters," the man in
the kitchen said, "it ought to be twenty. It'll have to be
done again." So he scratched it out and wrote "twenty
liters" and I went back to the corporal for a new
voucher. I couldn't understand it and kept shaking my
head and saying to myself: "How on earth are they
going to give us twenty liters of milk in a place like
this?" Well, they sent me from one place to another,
until finally I got back, empty-handed, to the yard
beneath my cell. Then, as I passed under it, the boys
tipped a bucket of water on top of me and soaked me to
the skin! Fortunately, my mother came soon after and I
changed my clothes. I didn't mind the joke; I knew my
own turn would come soon. So I said to the corporal in
charge: "Well, Corp, things don't seem to be going on
too well here!" He laughed and said: "Well, that should
teach you not to be such a fool next time."

The boys were new to me. I didn't know any of them,
except one: we called him The Turk. He had a basket of
fruit and pastries, which he tried to keep locked up; but
we always got at them. He was about seventeen, I think.
He'd gone off with some of his employer's cash: he was
in for fraud. Another boy was Argentine. We called him
Sewer Rat, as he had a tremendous appetite. He ate up
everyone's food, never left a crumb. He was extremely

thin, but a great eater. Fair-haired; only fifteen. He'd
been caught with three others breaking into cars: a boy
called Mackay, another one I nicknamed The Little
German, and a small child of five whom they used to
slip through the car window to open it up from inside.
He was a very tiny boy. Then there was a boy who
didn't stay long, whom we called Dynamite Kid. He
had a marvelous body, which he used to exercise a lot.
He was seventeen and had a fiancée. He's in here now,
as a matter of fact. Then there was a boy—I don't
remember his name—who used to sell *empanadas* on
the beach. One day he was hungry and ate them all
himself! That was why he was in: theft. Then there was
Cyanide: his language was so filthy; and a boy we
called The Despot. He was very white-skinned, with
thin, delicate hands, like a woman's, and he wore
glasses. Quite white he was—no color in his face at all;
sixteen or seventeen. His father had money, and he
treated us as if we were his vassals, wanting us all to
bow down before him. He had been arrested with his
father for smuggling jewelry. He showed us a clipping
about him in the paper. Then there was Lucho, who was
dark with a pockmarked face; and Panther, who had a
mobile, slithery body; and Nat King Cole, black like a
Negro; and a boy we called Chief, who never spoke to
anyone. I was nicknamed El Mocho, but they couldn't
pronounce it properly and used to say *Maucho. Mocho*
means someone with a physical deformity—in my case
they called me this because of my two missing fingers.
The boys were poor, but they all had families who

visited them and brought them food. That's about it. I
liked them mostly—they were decent fellows, and in
the forty-eight days I was with them I got along well
with them. They were fellows like me. The others didn't
know what a *carreta* was, but I did: so five of us got
together and formed one. We had all got mugs and a
pot and kettle between us, and I asked my *mamá* to
bring me a spirit stove to cook on. From then on, we had
our meals together.

That night, New Year's Eve, I was sent food from
home—a cooked goose, fresh fruit, biscuits, raisin bread,
pan de Pascua. We all chipped in that day, all the boys
made a great pile of the food and things they had been
sent, and we put it on the table, which had a tablecloth
that day (I don't know who brought that), and at
eleven that night we sat down to a meal. But we all felt
very depressed that New Year's. I kept thinking about
my *mamá* and family and about Gaby, and I kept
hoping that the guards would let my *mamá* come and
visit me tomorrow. Sometimes they let people in, if they
liked them. We passed the time chatting about different
adventures we had had. One boy, who was fifteen, told
us that he had fallen in love with his boss' daughter and
had been fired for it; another told us about a fight he
had been in; others about their trips—to the north or
south of Chile, or to Argentina; another boy told us
about smuggling. We all had some story to tell. Then
some of the boys sneaked off to their bunks and cried a
little.

It was very depressing. A little before midnight the

warders changed shift; the new warder on duty, who was a little drunk, looked through the peephole at us and tried to cheer us up. He said we looked more like a funeral and offered to lend us a portable radio, but he couldn't open our cell door. In the end, we had to use a piece of wire to open it ourselves, and then he passed us the set. Well, that cheered us up a lot. We made a sort of claret with the fruit juice we had in the cell, and started eating again and dancing among ourselves to the music from the radio. When we got too tired, we just left everything any old way and went to sleep.

I was all combed and ready next day for visiting hours when I heard the guards calling my name. I thought it was going to be my *mamá* but it turned out to be some of the gang, and Gaby with them. She gave me a hug, and asked me what I had got out of all this. The fellows had brought me some large food parcels. They all said they would come back and see me later, but they never did. The second visit was my Aunt Gloria and a girl who came with her. She brought an enormous package of food for me from my *mamá*—there were all sorts of things in it, cheese, bread, *pan de Pascua,* and some fruit. I tossed the stuff on my bed and gave her back the bag. My aunt told me that the señora was quite right to have had me arrested; it would teach me a lesson. "All right," I said, "but there's no need to go on about it. Isn't it enough that I'm here?" Then she said she would do what she could for me. The third visit was from my *mamá* and brother; the last from a friend I knew, a boy. At the end of these visits I went back to the

cell and started eating the fruit I had been brought, and
smoking. I noticed that some of my apples had walked.

Apart from the New Year, nothing much happened in
the month and a half I was in here the first time. Just the
usual routine. We'd go down in the mornings to get
water to make ourselves tea or coffee for breakfast; then
we'd clean out the cell and wash down the passageways.
At eleven the "house breakfast" appeared—beans: some
of the boys didn't eat them. They preferred to eat what
they had been brought from outside. Then we messed
around in the yard till one o'clock, when we were
locked in for an hour to give the guards time for their
lunch. At two we were let out again to the yard. On
Tuesdays we played volleyball; on Thursdays a movie;
otherwise, we amused ourselves playing checkers or
ludo. Our cell was quite clean and comfortable, and we
had two blankets each—one old, one new. Everyone
had to keep his blankets clean himself. The sergeant
used to come around to inspect them; twice a week we
gave them a good shaking outside. And the health
people used to come around once a week to disinfect
them. They don't come around any more now. The cell
had a couple of benches, a table, and a chair in it, but
we weren't supposed to put anything up on the walls.
We didn't have anything then; but actually they do
allow you to put up pictures—of actors and actresses,
for instance. I've even got a picture of that artiste, who
became a woman—Coccinelli! The walls in that cell,
though, were bare—just scratches and scrawls, "So-
and-so was here," that kind of thing. We didn't have

anywhere to keep our things; but then, what's the point? I've never lost anything here—except fruit: you always eat other people's fruit, if you're hungry. Even the last time I never lost anything—except the clothes I came in: the white sweater with black stripes and the jeans I had on when I was arrested.

Things went on like this until the day I was released. Then quite unexpectedly one morning I was called over to the Juvenile Court. A young lady asked me my name and why I had been arrested. "For larceny," I said. "What did you steal?" she asked. "A razor," I replied. "Who did you steal it from?" "I don't remember." "Well, you are free now," she said, "we are taking you home." "Have you got anything in the Detention Center?" Well, I had asked someone to look after my things when I was called to court, as I suspected I might be released. It was just a precaution, as I wasn't sure: just in case. Now I did not dare to go back for them, in case they wouldn't let me out. So I said: "No, nothing," and lost them all.

A detective came to take me home. All the way he kept trying to give me advice. I ought to work, or study, and not get into any more trouble, he said. "Look at me, I work as a detective in the daytime and go to school at night." He talked a lot of rot! I just let it wash over me.

When I reached home, I called out to my mother, who left her washing and came racing down the steps to hug me. She started to cry. My mother was wearing an old, patched dress, and I think the detective felt ashamed of all the nonsense he had talked to me when he saw how poor my *mamá* was. But in any case, I was too old to be given such advice. He just said: "Señora, look after your son," and pushed off. When I went inside, I found my Aunt Anita cooking. She also hugged me and cried and told me not to get into any more trouble. Then she went on with her work. My Granny came into the house when she heard my aunt call out: "Look, we've got visitors!" She was very pleased to see me: even my dog Pinocho, came to my side. Then I went out to play with my little cousins, who had just returned from school.

At lunch my mother asked me if I thought of looking for a job. I said I didn't know yet. My aunt said that she thought she might find me something through a friend who worked in her factory. She is a seamstress. In the end, they said I should wait a few days anyway. That night I went to watch some wrestling in the Arab Sporting Club with the boys and I didn't get home till one in the morning; I slept until midday. My Aunt Gloria commented on this at lunch, and said it was time for me to get hold of a newspaper and start looking for a job. My Granny said she thought she could help me through a friend she knew at her work in the laundry. Well, she asked the friend, who knew a man who had a shop, and I got a job serving at the counter. It was a shop that sold cooking utensils, furniture, clothes, shoes, all that sort of thing. I worked there throughout March. I was tired of drifting around doing nothing; after work I used to go straight home—I never went out at all. I liked the job too; they were very polite—they used to address me as Señor.

On the last Saturday of the month, a customer came in to buy a pair of shoes. He wanted a cheap pair, so I got him out some, and he finally chose a pair he liked. Unfortunately, I didn't know much about shoes, and muddled up the boxes they were in, so when he asked me the price of the pair he had chosen I got it wrong, and gave him a good pair for the price of a cheap one. Of course, I didn't know this at the time; I just made out the bill for him, wrapped them up, and went on with my work. About half an hour later, the owner of the shop called me over and asked me what sales I had made. He used to put down each sale in a ledger. When I told him the number of the box of shoes I had sold, he was furious with me. He bawled me out good and proper, called me a fool and a thief, deducted the difference from my pay and fired me on the spot. The difference represented a whole week's work for me, but there was nothing I could do about it, so I took what he gave me and left.

When I got home and told my mother what had happened, she shrugged her shoulders and said I had better look for something else. Early in April I found another job as apprentice in the turner's workshop I had been in two years earlier, in 1959, when I was still living with my Aunt Berta. The pay was four or five escudos a week—depending on the hours. The owner was very strict about this. If you arrived ten minutes late, he deducted the minutes from your pay. Of course, if you

worked overtime he paid you more as well. In my
second week there—Holy Week, it was—he sent me
across to the post office to change a fifty-escudo
banknote. Well, I don't know what came over me, but
just as I was coming back to the shop with the change I
thought better of it, and ran away with the money. I
went home first to get a bag and some clothes quickly
before the Investigaciones were notified; I didn't want
to bump into the detectives who'd be certain to be sent
to get me. My mother was surprised to see me so early in
the day, but I told her that I had been sent by the owner
to Santiago and had to be away for a week or so. I don't
know why I took the money; I had no idea how I was
going to spend it, but I didn't think I'd be caught. The
police wouldn't bother to scour the entire city in search
of a measly fifty escudos. For them it would just be
another of the hundreds of thefts reported to the
Investigaciones during the day, I thought. I went and
had my hair cut, had ham and eggs at a café, bought
myself a couple of magazines and a Superman comic,
and sat down to read them in the Plaza Victoria. Then
to a matinee till six; back to the plaza in the evening to
meet the gang; then dancing in the Pérgola Cancan. I
met a schoolgirl called Eva there; I told her she had
made a hit with me, that she was very attractive—you
know the sort of things you say to a girl when you want
to flirt. She didn't say anything, just blushed. She was a
pretty girl, with pretty eyes and light brown hair; the
right height for me, and quite slender. By about nine I'd
got bored with the dancing and wanted to leave. I was

paying for everything, so the gang had to leave too. On the way home with Eva, I led her down a side alley, took her in my arms, and started kissing her. She promised to be my girl so long as I kept quiet about it to the gang. The jokes in the plaza can be pretty nasty, and she didn't want people carrying tales back to her *mamá*. Afterwards, while I was drifting around the dock area, with nowhere to go, I saw quite an attractive tart standing outside the Hotel Duque and invited her to have supper with me in the Cachás Grandes. (She must have been about twenty.)

"Got any money?" she asked me.

"Enough for supper for the two of us," I said.

"All right, I accept—but no monkey tricks, mind."

While we were waiting to be served, a drunken sailor stumbled across us on his way to the Gents and fell on the tart's lap.

"Please leave the young lady alone, señor," I said.

"Just an accident," he explained, so no more was said. But after supper, just as we were on our way out, a stevedore grabbed me by the arm and said: "Here's the young fellow who was trying to pick a fight just now!"

I don't know why he should have said that, but I replied, coolly: "You are mistaken, señor."

"Push off, you twerp," the man said to me, "you're too young to be worth bothering with!"

The tart took my arm and started steering me away. "Come on," she said, "don't waste your time on him!"

When we had shaken off the man and were out in the

street again, she said to me: "It's bedtime now." I
agreed.

"What hotel would you recommend?"

"You can come back with me, if you like," she said.
"I've got a room in the Brooklyn."

"What are you going to charge?" I asked.

"Five escudos for an all-night stand." This was very
cheap.

"Fine. Let's go then."

In the hotel bedroom, I looked out of the window
while the tart got undressed. There was a street fight
going on outside—a gang of pickpockets having a free-
for-all, using knives. Quite a lot of people were watching; from where I was, I could see the police van on its
way to round them up. I shut the window; what did it
matter to me? By the time I had turned round, the tart
was practically undressed. I went up to her and gave
her a kiss.

"My God, you're pushed!" she said.

"What do you mean?" I said, "I've got all night,
haven't I?"

She climbed into bed, leaving plenty of room for me,
and said briefly: "Come to bed!" She was only wearing a
nightie and a pair of panties.

I undressed, took my money out of my trouser
pockets—I had about thirty-five escudos on me—and
hid it under the lining of my jacket. I was very suspicious of her. Then I slipped in beside her. When I'd
finished my cigarette, I started kissing and rubbing
up against her.

"Take my panties off first," she said. I did this.

"Now take off your own."

She lifted up her nightdress and we had relations. When we had finished, she wanted a soft drink. "You can get it from the woman downstairs, who 'married' us," she said. So I went down—wearing nothing but my trousers and jacket—to order a cuba libre for myself and a soft drink for the girl. They charged me one and a half escudos, which I thought very expensive.

I slept soundly till five in the morning, when the girl rolled over in her sleep onto me. This woke us both up, so she took me in her arms and kissed me. She kept murmuring how nice I was, how different from the other boys who drifted around the docks. We had relations again. After that, I read a magazine for a bit and dozed off for an hour or so, when she made me get up and have a wash. I looked to see if my money was still there; I found it was, and asked her how much I owed her. "Nothing," she said. She refused the five escudos for a bit, but I insisted and tucked it in the pocket of her blouse; she kept it in the end. Then she kissed me goodbye and told me to come back and see her again. I spent the morning on the beach; in the afternoon I went to a matinee—an Italian picture, "The Nights of Cabiria." An excellent picture, very interesting, about a gang of *ponces* who exploit a girl and then try to kill her. In the end she marries a fellow with money. I went dancing again that evening, with the boys. Eva was there; but somehow I didn't enjoy it much. I also bumped into my brother in the plaza. He

hadn't heard yet about what I had done; he asked me
how my mother and everyone was at home and what I
was now doing. I made up some lies. He was living with
my Aunt Berta—he still is—and attending night school.
I slept that night in a room with six or seven other beds
in a flophouse. I had a bed to myself, which was quite
clean.

Next day, while I was sitting in the street reading
some Mickey Mouse comics, I felt someone touch my
shoulder from behind and say: "That's him, all right." It
was the boy who worked with me in the turner's shop.
He was with a policeman.

"Your papers, young fellow," he said.

"I haven't any," I replied.

"You are under arrest for stealing fifty escudos. Have
you anything to say?"

"I don't know anything about it."

"Well, come along with me."

I tried to slip out of my jacket and run away, but the
cop was too quick for me. He grabbed my arm, twisted
it behind my back, and marched me off to the police
station. They put me in a cell by myself. It turned out
that the boy had seen me from a bus he was in and had
gone to find a policeman. I didn't mind; I wasn't mad at
him or anything. Like last time, I couldn't sleep at all
that night; I kept pacing up and down in the cell, alone.
Next morning they took me to the Detention Center and
put me back in the Juveniles section. The corporal was
still there; he was sergeant now. He stared at me but
said nothing. The boys in the cell all crowded around

me asking for cigarettes, questioning me about why I was in. They tried the old "milk" trick on me again, but I told them I knew that one; after that, they left me alone. The boys were a different bunch this time; the old ones had gone.

After a couple of weeks I got a job as a waiter in the Detention Center *pensionado* for the well-to-do prisoners. Here, you know, there are two *pensionados;* one for the poor, which is free, and another where you have to pay. A bed costs two hundred pesos a night, plus one escudo for meals. It's one and a half escudos now; the price has gone up. You don't have to do any of the work yourself there, and it's cleaner and more comfortable.

Well, just before I'd done four months in here, a woman friend of my mother's came to see me and told me that my Aunt Gloria had bribed the law clerk to get me bail. I thought she was having me on, and told her to go away and leave me alone. That evening I remember washing the plates, half-hoping that what she said was true, but by seven o'clock I began to lose heart. But sure enough, a little later the court did send for me; I had been granted bail and was now free. I ran down the stairs from the courtroom, collected my things from the Center, and met my aunt and the señora who had told me that I was to be set free, who had been waiting all the time outside for me. As we walked off home, I heard a woman calling me from behind. "Don't look back," my aunt said, "it's unlucky!" But I didn't catch what she said, and looked back. It was a mother asking me if her son had come out that day. He hadn't; I was the last to

be released. On the way home I passed Eva, but she
didn't recognize me, and a little later I saw several boys
and girls I knew. They stared at me at first, but then
they greeted me quite normally. I expect they realized
when they saw me with my aunt, carrying so many
packages and pots and pans, that I was just out of
prison.

In the next few weeks nothing much happened. It
was decided that I shouldn't try to get a job before the
Fiestas Patrias (September 18). I used to get up late,
wander around the hill, drop in on a friend of my Aunt
Gloria's who had three daughters, all of them pretty.
The one I liked best had got into trouble and had a
baby; she was about twenty, I think. The other two
were younger.

On the eve of Dieciocho (September 18), my *mamá*
threw a party; there was food, wine, music—the works.
Quite a lot of girls were invited. One of them was called
María Elena. She was small, and very attractive; but I
didn't get around to dancing with her till midnight,
when I stayed on talking to her in the sitting room. My
mother was playing cards in a corner there, so I ended
by taking her outside in the yard. We talked about
music: I said I liked classical music—operas like "Aida"
and "La Traviata," which I had heard on records with
my brother; we talked about movies. I asked her all
sorts of questions about herself; then I kissed her. But I
was called inside by my mother, who said it was time
the guests started leaving. We began collecting the
plates. It was two in the morning.

Next day, Dieciocho, I arranged to go with Pablo to
the improvised open-air cafés, *fondas*, in Playa Ancha. I
wanted to invite the girl I had met the night before, and
we went to her house to ask her, but she wouldn't come.
At the *fondas* we went in for some of the competitions,
and I won a can of peaches. So we bought a liter of wine
at a café, poured it in, and drank it. But the wine went
to my head very quickly, and I started fooling around
with an air rifle at one of the stands, waving it about,
shooting it up in the air, and causing a terrible commo-
tion. Quite a crowd gathered. When the cops came,
they took both of us behind one of the *fondas*, gave us a
couple of slaps on the face, chucked some cold water
over us, and sobered us up. They told us to go on home.
It was about one in the morning by now, and we took
their advice. As we hadn't any money and it was too far
to walk, the only thing to do was to hitch a ride on the
back of a bus. I scrambled on the top of one, and Pablo
hung on to the back. But when it stopped in Bellavista
Station, I didn't have time to get off. By the time I had
walked back, Pablo had gone to sleep on the curb! We
struggled home somehow, but I fell right over the fence
into the flowerbed, and that's where they found me next
morning. My Granny was furious with me. "Look at this
drunk," she said, "he's gone and spoiled all my flowers!"
I crawled into bed with Pablo, who was asleep with all
his clothes on, and didn't wake up till midday. I had
an awful hangover.

Next day, as everyone had gone back to work, I was
at a loose end. I thought of calling on my grandmother

and went to see her, but my Aunt Berta, who was at
home, hardly spoke to me, and I refused to go and greet
my uncle. They have always had it in for me. So I didn't
stay long. In the end, I wandered off in the direction of
the Commercial School, where I used to go, and arrived
just in time to meet various fellows I knew coming out. I
played football with them for a while, but got bored and
went to the matinee instead. It was a Mexican picture in
a round-the-clock movie. That's the beauty of those
places. You can just sit there, killing time, coming out
very late. When I got home, my mother asked me if I
had found work. "I'll start looking tomorrow," I said.
Then I remembered I'd lost my identity card at the
fondas, and said I'd have to get a new one first. My
mother accused me of looking for excuses for not
working. So September and October passed—without a
job. There were jobs available for three or four escudos
a week, sweeping floors, that sort of thing; but nothing
suitable for me. I wanted work at a counter in a soda
fountain, or as a baker's assistant—that kind of thing
brings you in about twenty escudos a week. But nothing
doing.

With November 1—the Day of the Dead—looming
up, my cousin suggested we might go to the cemetery
and make a killing, filling flower jars on the graves with
water for the old women who came that day. They give
you as much as one escudo in tips, and you can make
even more by stealing bunches of flowers—carnations,
for instance—from the graves and selling them to the
new arrivals. I said I'd think about it, but he turned on

me at once. "Don't think about it," he said, "just come. I'll take the ladder for the high niches; you can take along those big twenty-kilo cans—the kind used for lard."

Next morning we got up at four and went to the cemetery. The stands were opening up as we arrived and people were busy arranging their flowers for sale, but the cemetery gates were not yet open, and we were told to get into line with the *pelusas* and other boys who had had the same idea as us. I had put on all my oldest clothes—torn cap, patched pants, old shirt; the only thing I had on that was any good was a pair of dark glasses. I wasn't going to be recognized by someone I knew and laughed at. Soon a lady passed and asked us for a ladder and some water. Then another and another: hundreds rolled up. By lunchtime we had made about seven or eight escudos each. In the afternoon I suddenly saw Silvia. She was wearing a brown check dress, beads, a white nylon jersey, and a Jacqueline Kennedy hairstyle. Now, I had my oldest things on, but I didn't mind that—she had often seen me looking like that before. But I looked down; it hurt me to see her, and I went on with my job.

At the end of the day we counted up how much we had made. I had nineteen escudos; Pablo said he had fourteen escudos. He didn't want to tell me how much he had, in case I told his mother; he used to give her his earnings. This time he wanted to keep something for himself. It stood to reason he had made more than I did—the boy with the ladder always makes more—and

I told him I wouldn't let on, but he didn't tell me all the same.

A few days later, Pablo said he had found me a job in a bakery. I had all my papers now—identity card, clean police record (a forged one, of course), and they took me on. I was going to get five escudos a week for the first month as an apprentice, and about fifteen escudos after that. Don Cito, the boss, gave me a flour sack to have made up into an apron at home and told me to bring soap to wash my face and hands before starting work. He asked me if I had money to buy any; I said "Yes." I hadn't, actually, but I remembered I had bought a piece of scented soap once which I had never used, I could take that. Well, time passed; I learned how to knead, bake, make pastries, cakes—all that stuff. I liked the work, and learned quickly; it wasn't heavy work, either. By December I was doing overtime and making twenty escudos weekly. I got along with the others too; never had any trouble with them at all. There were two girls there I remember; we were good friends, all three of us got along with the owner and his wife. Sometimes on Fridays I used to go to their house to help them chop up the onions for the *empanadas,* which I delivered to different places on Saturday. They let you eat whatever you liked in the bakery too; there were no restrictions.

We had a very quiet Christmas. I went off again like the year before to Don Anselmo's snack bar, but there was no one I knew there, no friend, and I got fed up with drinking by myself, so I just went home again. When I got back I found my stepfather had left me a present, a pair of bedroom slippers. I didn't see him, as usual. He works as a lineman on the railroad in Llay-Llay and only comes home on public holidays. He doesn't stay, goes back the same night. All the same, we had a very good New Year's. My mother, Granny, and aunt had all clubbed together and bought me some beautiful eighteen-carat-gold cuff links and a gold tiepin with a little golf bag attached to it. I cried a little and asked them why they had spent so much money on me. Then I invited them all to come out with me for a party. But my Granny didn't want to go out, so Pablo and I went off to buy things for a party at home instead. We got three kilos of meat from a new butcher's which had just opened near us; plenty of wine, Coca-Cola, cakes, sweets, everything. My mother prepared the roast, my aunt made the salads, the rest of us opened the wine and served it around to all the people who had come in to see us. As the three kilos of meat wasn't enough, we sent out for another five, which we roasted on a fire outside in the yard. That's how I spent New Year's: very good fun it was. Pablo and I paid for it all between us.

That first month of the new year 1962 there was a carnival in Quilpué, which I used to go to every day after work with friends. I stayed every night till midnight, whooping it up and dancing with the girls. In February there was another one, even better, called the Carioca—something like the one in Río de Janeiro; well, not so big or nice as that, of course, but still . . . I went there with a friend from the bakery: it was *macanudo*,

real great. On the day it opened I was wearing some
new clothes my brother had given me: a sports jacket
with gray and black stripes, beautiful it was, like the
kind you see in the movies, very short below the waist. I
wore it with a pair of black trousers, a silk handkerchief,
and a tiepin I borrowed from Pablo. I looked the cat's
whiskers, I can tell you! Well, while we were watching a
number on the dance floor, with everyone pushing and
shoving to see, I found myself next to a couple of girls.
One of them was dark, but the other was fair-haired,
with green eyes, very pretty. The shoving went on and
on, and I lost sight of the boy I was with; all this time I
kept eyeing the blonde beside me and hanging on to
her—to keep her from being knocked down in the
crush, you understand. After a while I got fed up.

"Why don't we get out of here?" I asked her. "I'll
come with you, if you like."

The girl thought this funny and burst out laughing.
"I'm with friends," she said.

"Make up some story and give them the slip," I suggested.

She looked over her shoulder. When she saw they
were looking the other way, she took my hand in hers
and we made our escape to an open-air dance floor. We
danced to a song I liked that was very popular at the
time, "La Pelotita," in the center of the floor; the other
dancers made a circle around us. Quite a lot of people
were in fancy dress; and a bunch of queers dressed up
as women were dancing with men. There were a lot of
jokes from the crowd, and horsing around—it was all

very funny, but Marcela didn't like being mixed up with them, and made me dance with her on the edge of the floor at the back. After the dance, we strolled off to a kiosk where I bought some pasties for her. As she said she was not going steady with anyone, I asked her to be my girl. Then I took her in my arms and kissed her, but she moved away and said it was time to catch the train back to Viña. She nestled up against me on the train, as she was cold, and I lent her my coat; she fell asleep on my shoulder. She wouldn't let me see her home, so I had to leave her at the bottom of the hill in Forestal Alto, where she lived. Before kissing her good night, I asked her when I could see her again. "In two weeks' time," she said. So we arranged to meet in the Viña Plaza on March 4.

The day before I was due to keep my date, I was fired from the bakery. Don Cito caught me using the phone to make a private call: I was calling a girl I had met in the Feria del Mar (a public exhibition in a Viña park). He told me to leave next day, but at the time I didn't take this seriously, as he'd often been annoyed with me before and he was in a bad mood that day. I thought it'd just blow over. I appeared next day for work as usual. But I was wrong. This time he meant it. At midday he paid me off and sent me packing. I didn't mind much, to tell you the truth. I'd been working there nearly four months and was getting bored. When I left, I said to the boss: "Goodbye, Don Cito, please excuse me for all the trouble I've caused you."

I spent the afternoon before my date getting ready

for it. I put on a pair of light trousers, Prince of Wales
check, and a double-breasted blazer with gilt buttons,
and told my mother I was off to the carnival to have a
look around. I arrived in the plaza a little early, so I
messed around a bit, bought myself a Walt Disney
comic, and lit up a cigarette to wait. I was reading it
through for the second time when Marcela arrived.
"Tired of waiting, Cristián?" she said. She always
called me Cristián; I never like giving a girl my real
name when I meet her for the first time. "Not at all, I've
only just got here myself," I said. We spent the evening
at the carnival again. It couldn't have been better. We
arranged to meet in the plaza again next day.

I was especially looking forward to this meeting
because she had promised to take me home and intro-
duce me to her parents. I arrived at 6:30 sharp and
waited for her. Well, seven o'clock struck, then half
past, eight, eight-thirty, and still there were no signs of
her. I felt very fed up. I didn't know her address, so all
I could do was walk to where I used to say good night to
her, in the hope of seeing her about. When I got there, I
couldn't find her anywhere, so there was nothing to do
but go back again to the plaza in case she had turned up
in the meantime, and I had missed her. But of course
she wasn't there. Then I suddenly remembered she had
said she might not be able to get out that evening to
keep her date as her *papá* might not let her. If that
happened, she said, I was to wait for her in the Plaza of
Forestal Alto at nine, when she came down to fetch the
bread. That meant I was late for the appointment, and I

had to race back in a taxi to reach the other plaza on time. I had been waiting there for about ten minutes without any result when a girl passed me. It was the girl who had been with Marcela in the carnival the first time I had seen her. She knew where Marcela lived, so she pointed out the house to me. As I was walking toward it, some girls who were playing in the street outside began whistling the tune of the song Marcela and I had danced to that time in Quilpué, "La Pelotita." As I turned to look at them, I saw Marcela. She was wearing very narrow, light blue trousers, a woollen sweater, and a blue jacket; I didn't like her getup at all, far too flashy.

"Marcela," I said, "have you forgotten all about me?"

"I couldn't get away; my father's out."

"What about your mother? Isn't she at home?"

"Just got in this minute," she said. "Why, I haven't even been down for the bread!"

I believed her and accepted her apology. But it was ten o'clock now, and I had to leave. She walked with me to the bus stop.

"When can I see you again?" I asked.

"Tomorrow, at half past six," she said. "Over there." She pointed to a lamp post not far from the stop. I took her in my arms and kissed her. As I got into the bus, "six-thirty tomorrow, then," she said, "don't forget."

Pablo was waiting up for me at eleven, when I got home, to tell me that he had found me a job at a grocer's. It was going to be hard work, but well paid.

"As long as the pay is good," I told him, "you can let the *patrona* know I'll take it on."

"I'm taking you myself to meet her first thing in the morning," he said. "You'll have to be up bright and early: we've got to be out by six."

Next morning I woke all right, but I couldn't get Pablo up. He just swore at me, turned over, and went to sleep again. In the end I got a jug of water and poured it over him. Then he did get up.

We arrived at the grocer's just as it was opening. Pablo introduced me to Don José and Doña Raquel, the owners of the shop, as the cousin he had talked to them about, and told them I had just lost my job in a bakery. All my papers were in order and I had recommendations as well. Don José began to make some inquiries.

"What schooling have you got?"

"I finished second year secondary school," I said.

"Got a certificate or anything to prove it?"

"No, but you can test me by giving me a sum to do."

"You've got to be able to handle money and work out accounts," he said. "Then there's all the bookkeeping side—you've got to learn to do all that. The hours are till half past eight. Do you go to night school?"

I remembered my date that evening with Marcela, so I said I had classes every day at six. That would just give me time.

"That's all right," he said, "you can leave at a quarter to six each day. There's never much doing after six." I started work at once.

That same afternoon a girl came into the shop to buy

some vegetables. Pretty as a doll, she was—though a bit *pituca*, rather affected. She turned out to be the niece of Doña Raquel—and of Doña Marta, the señora I'd stolen the razor from the previous year. The family had quite a bit of money. Well, when the girl saw me working there she protested: "Aunt Raquel, how can you have people like that working in the shop? How on earth can you take people on without making any inquiries about them?" Fortunately, the señora didn't take in what her niece said—at least, she let her remarks pass over her without comment. But the girl kept staring at me as I attended to her order—she stared so hard that she made me embarrassed, and I lowered my eyes. It was only then that, as I glanced down at my clothes, I realized what a sight I looked. I don't know when I've been so poorly dressed and dirty. But it wasn't this so much that made me feel ashamed. It was more that this girl, standing there, sneering, in front of me, should know my secret. It made me mad, I can tell you; and I was as surly to her as I dared to be. In fact, I practically threw the goods across the counter at her—making sure of course that her aunt didn't see. You won't believe me, but that girl leaned across the counter and said to me, under her breath: "I suppose you'll only take advantage of your position here to steal from my aunt! I'm afraid she's not very bright."

I glared at her. Then with the same nasty look on her face she turned her back on me and walked out of the shop. Here I was, then, working hard, doing everything I could to earn my bosses' trust, wanting to get on and be given a more responsible job, to earn more; and this girl comes along to mess it all up for me!

As luck would have it, I ran into her after work that day. The señora had let me leave at a quarter to six, and I was hurrying to the corner to catch the bus to Viña to keep my date when I saw her.

I went up to her and said straight out: "Señorita," I said, "you don't know what I went through in the month and a half I spent in prison for stealing from your aunt. What I did to your aunt I paid for, believe me—dearly. And I even paid her back the money for her razor. She can't have anything against me now. Can't you see that I am trying to go straight? Please don't try and wreck it all for me now."

"I'm sorry," she said, "I didn't mean it that way. I only thought you wanted to pinch from my aunt. By the way, are you on your way to school now?" "Yes," I said. I had told her aunt that morning that I was going to school, so I had to go on with the lie.

"What year are you in?"

"Third," I told her. I had started in the third year in the Commercial School, though I had given it up.

"I could easily get permission from my aunt for you to leave work early, you know," she went on. "Then you could come over to my house for half an hour or so in the afternoon; I might be able to help you with your homework."

She was sixteen, I think. I believe she was in the sixth year in secondary school. I thanked her and said I appreciated her kindness.

"Please don't go on calling me señorita," she said. "I know I'm a bit *pituca,* but that doesn't mean I'm not just an ordinary girl. Are we friends now?" she asked, and she held out her hand to me. We shook hands.

I waited more than half an hour for Marcela, but she never turned up, so I had to go up to the house. As I got within sight of it, a gentleman came out of the door with two small girls. As they passed me on their way to a soda fountain, I could hear the youngest child say: "Look, Papá, there's the boy who went up the hill last night hand in hand with Marcela!" The gentleman glanced quickly at me, but I crossed the road, pretending to look for someone on the other side, and lit up a cigarette. I waited a while, then I followed them into the soda fountain. The little girl was asking for some sweets, but her *papá* said he didn't have any money to buy them, so I turned to him and politely offered to buy them for her. He accepted; I saw he was a bit drunk.

"Waiting for Marcela?" he asked. "She's not back from work yet," he added.

We got talking. I told him where I was working, what school I had been to, and said that Marcela and I were going steady now. He invited me back to his home to wait for Marcela there.

When she arrived, they asked me to have supper with them, so I sent out for some *chicha,* and Coca-Cola for the children. We had a party. I danced with Marcela; we played records, had a very good time. Don José—her *papá*—said we looked very nice together: we'd make a fine married couple, he said! Well, by eleven o'clock I

was beginning to feel sick with all that *chicha,* and
Marcela had said she had something very important to
tell me—outside. Well, when she walked with me to the
bus stop afterwards, she still hadn't said anything. I
tried to kiss her, but she slapped me on the face.

"What's up?" I asked. I couldn't understand it.

"Nothing," she said. "It's just that I've met another
boy I like better than you, so I'm going steady with him.
That's what I wanted to tell you."

"I hope you aren't sore with me," she went on. "You
told me yourself, you know, that if I found someone
else. . . ."

"I know I did," I said. "Well, that's it then. Goodbye."
So I left her and went into a bar in town and drank until
two in the morning. I had to walk home.

Next evening after my second day of work in the
grocer's, I had nowhere to go. I was messing around at
loose ends when I recognized a woman I knew slightly
by sight. She used to come to visit a man in jail when I
was there in 1961. She was a girl, really—about eighteen, I should think. As the man was over thirty, I took it
for granted she was his sister. Well, I accosted her and
tried to get into conversation, but she wasn't having any
and moved away. So I followed her, talking. I mentioned I had been in jail with her brother. "He wasn't
my brother," she said, "he was my husband." She was
interested now, so I started telling her about the theft of
money from the workshop which put me inside that
time. "We all do silly things," she said. She told me her

name: María. We went on talking. I told her where I
was working, and said that I had fought with my
girl.

"I used to fight with my boyfriend too," she said,
"before I got married."

"Don't give me that stuff about being married, María,"
I said to her—and took her hand. She kept her eyes
downcast, so I took her in my arms and kissed her. She
was a little unwilling at first, but then she kissed me
back. "Why did you do that?" she asked.

I liked her, I said. Wouldn't she be my girl? I had a
job, I wasn't just a bum who went around picking
women up.

"Come around tomorrow to the laundry where I
work," she said. "I'll give you my answer then."

As we were walking toward the dock area, she saw
her sister approaching with a boyfriend. "We'll have to
hide," she said. "I can't have my sister seeing me around
with you here." We hurried on till we came to an open
doorway, and hid inside until they had passed. Then I
had to take her home.

Next day at work there was trouble about a check.
Don José had taken his check book out of the safe to pay
one of the truck drivers in the morning, but in the
afternoon, when he came to open his safe again, he
found a check was missing. He couldn't understand it,
and asked me if I had seen one lying around anywhere
in the shop. I hadn't. As a matter of fact, I didn't even
know it had been lost, until he told me.

"You didn't take it yourself, I suppose?" he asked.

"How could I?" I said. "You're the one who always keeps the safe keys."

Nothing more was said about it then.

Now, that morning I had made friends with a girl called Magdalena who had come to the shop for some fruit. She was very pretty, with a well-built body, milk-white skin, brown-green eyes, and lovely black hair; she was my own age, and the right height. After work I ran into her again on her way to buy a comic at the corner, wearing a pink dress, with a rather low neck, and a rose at her breast. I had been wondering whether to look María up—the girl I had met the previous night. Now I thought I'd invite Magdalena for a drink.

"No, thank you," she said. "But why don't we go to the Fun Fair in the Plaza O'Higgins? Do let's go and have a look at it!"

There were all sorts of things there. The great wheel, which she didn't want to go on, and merry-go-rounds and those whirling seats that go all over the place. Well, we went on one of those, and I kissed her while everyone was shouting and screaming, not noticing anything. The ticket man noticed us as we came out holding hands, calling each other *tú*, and gave me a peculiar look. He had seen us waiting our turn, in the line, treating each other very respectfully! Of course, by now I had completely forgotten about María.

Next day Doña Raquel's niece came into the shop to buy something, and asked me when I was going to take her up on her invitation to her home. For some reason I didn't feel much like work that day, I just wanted to mooch around the hill and go home early, so I invented an excuse and got permission from Doña Raquel to leave after three. I remember I left all my schoolbooks behind in the shop; I used to take them with me to the shop to keep up the pretense that I was going to night school.

As I was on my way home, I remembered there was a Mexican picture showing in town, called "Calibre 44," and I had enough money to get in. It was all about bandits. There was a good one and bad one, you see, and the bad one kills the good one, and then it turns out that the bad one is the good one and the good one the bad. *Macanudo*, real great it was! I didn't get home till ten or eleven at night. But when I went into my mother's bedroom to borrow a comic, she greeted me with: "Lord, child, what have you gone and done this time?"

"Done, Mamita?" I replied. "I haven't done anything. I've just come from the movies, that's all. Why, what's happened?"

"Well, the grocer's has sent the detectives after you. They say you've taken some checks."

"It's not true, Mamita," I said. "I haven't taken anything."

"You'd better go off to Investigaciones and tell them so," she said.

So that night I went to see them. "Don't worry, Mamita," I said to her, "I've nothing to fear."

When I got to Investigaciones, they told me they had

not received any complaint. It was probably some
mistake. They gave me a paper to sign, and I left. First
thing next morning I went to Señora Raquel and asked
her if she or Don José had put in a complaint about me
to the police. They hadn't, so I told them about the
detectives coming up to the house and my going to
Investigaciones that night.

"Did they arrest you?" she asked.

"Of course not," I said. "Otherwise, I wouldn't be
here."

So the matter rested there. Afterwards I found out
that it was Señora Raquel's sister-in-law who had put in
the complaint. She had heard that a check had been
mislaid and reported it, but when the police discovered
that she wasn't the injured party herself, they just tore it
up.

Mind you, I wasn't surprised or upset by all this.
Detectives from Investigaciones had been around to the
house on several occasions before. You see, whenever
there's a theft or robbery and they don't know who's
done it they just round up anyone with a police record,
on suspicion—as a matter of course. They've been
coming ever since I got out of jail the first time in 1961.
For instance, when I was working in the turner's workshop—a couple of days before I went off with the fifty
escudos, as a matter of fact—there'd been some robbery
in a shop downtown and the police thought I had been
hiding the goods at home. So they came and searched
the place. The other times I was working at the bakery:
someone had stolen from a shop across the street or

from a parked truck near the place; and once there was
a theft from a movie house. The police would come for
you about midnight and pull you in for questioning. I
was quite used to this, just routine!

A few days later, after I had completed a week's work
and been paid, I went to the Fun Fair with Magdalena
again. I was returning home when I saw a police truck
parked in front of the house. So I got off the road at once
and crept around by another path to within a few
yards of the house, from where I could hear what the
detectives were saying to my mother. They had come to
arrest me for the theft of that check, after all. When
they drove off, I went into my mother's bedroom.

"They're out looking for you," she said. "They want to
pull you in this time. They say they've got proof."

It was no good going to Investigaciones now. They'd
only have arrested me, and I'd have spent four or five
months inside before I could prove that I hadn't taken
the check. It wouldn't have been any use seeing Doña
Raquel either. If you've been in prison before, they're
bound to think you're the thief. I wasn't sure whether
they knew that I had been in jail, but they'd be told
soon enough. So there was nothing to do but disappear.
I put a few clothes in a suitcase and some money—
twenty escudos it was—and lit out that night. It was the
end of March, and I had nowhere to go. Then I
remembered Marcela. I was still on good terms with her
parents—and with her, if it came to that; I might be
able to stay with them, I thought. I'd pay for myself of
course. I didn't think of the time or anything, I just took

a bus and went there. Well, when I arrived the house was pitch dark, so I looked at my watch. It was one in the morning—much too late to burst in. In the excitement of the moment I'd just never noticed. I walked back to Viña and stayed the rest of the night in a hotel.

Next morning I bought some fish and fruit and vegetables as a present for Marcela's family and went to see them. Her mother opened the door.

"Come on in, Manolito," she said, "we haven't seen you for a long time."

"Mamita"—by the way, I had never called her Mamita before—"I've brought you a present," I said.

She invited me to lunch. While I was helping her slice the onions, she asked about Marcela and me. "We've quarreled," I said.

"Never mind. What have you got in your case?" I told her I had had a fight with my mother and had to leave home. She thought about this for a moment, then asked me to run out and buy some wine. "We'll talk about it afterwards," she said. When I came back with the wine—and some Coca-Cola for the children—she told me I could stay with them for a few days, until I'd made up with my *mamá,* and I gave her ten escudos toward my keep.

Don José and Marcela came to lunch but didn't stay afterwards, so Judith and I were left at home: we had nothing to do. "Why don't you two go off to the movies?" her *mamá* asked me. "Judith never goes out anywhere." So Judith changed into a short white dress with red flowers on it which came down to above the knee, and we left to see two Mexican pictures in town. She cut her evening classes in high school, so we went on afterwards to a café for a snack. That evening I bought all the girls sweets and we listened to the radio and put on records and played cards. I lent them money, but they didn't have any luck, and I nearly always won.

Next morning was a lovely, warm day and I wanted to go to the beach. (The family, by the way, thought I had the day off. Of course, I tried to dodge awkward questions.) "I'm going to get Judith up," I said to Mamita after breakfast, when the others had gone to work. "I'd like her to come to the beach with me." Mamita advised me to be careful of the sun and to be sure to put some suntan lotion on. We took their little radio with us. Now, Judith didn't know how to swim and hung around on the edge of the water paddling until I took her a little out of her depth and tried to show her. But she went under once or twice and wanted to go back, so I put my arm under her waist and swam with her to the shore. It's not at all difficult for me to do that, you understand. I don't know how many times in the past I have been pushed into a pool, fully dressed, while horsing around with the boys. I've also had plenty of practice trying to rescue fellows who've been thrown in for a lark and couldn't swim! We had a very good time on the beach. The only thing was that when we got back to lunch we found that sand had got into the radio, and it wouldn't work. In the afternoon I changed into a pair of charcoal-gray trousers, a black striped pullover, and a clean white shirt, and told Mamita that I was going into town and wouldn't be back till late.

In the dock area I bumped into a boy I knew, who asked me to go out on a job with him—go out robbing with him, he meant. I told him the detectives were out looking for me and I didn't want to run any risks.

"Look, I've got a diamond here, and there's a shop in Viña where you've only got to break the glass. It's a cinch. You're good at that. Why don't you do it for me? You won't get caught!"

He knew I used to break glass for fun when I was out in the Avenida Perú with the gang, and had never been caught. In the end, of course, he talked me into it. Besides, by now I had only about one escudo left.

So we waited for nightfall, eating snacks and chatting in the Cachás Grandes; but we failed. I don't know why, but I couldn't break the glass. So I went down the Avenida Libertad in search of someone to rob, some drunk. I planned to cosh him, a *cogoteo*.

Manuel in his narrative had now reached the crucial three weeks before his arrest for Mercier's murder. For some time he had been dawdling in our sessions. Now, on the eve, as it happened, of my departure from Valparaíso for a few weeks, he reached this point in his story at a single burst. Once he had arrived there, he seemed surprised and upset. "I cannot go on now. I must clear my mind and write it out first."

In the six months I had known him, he had never

made such a suggestion before. In the event, as the reader will see, Manuel was never to continue with his narrative under the same conditions. This does not mean that I did not learn the sequel—only that he was now caught up in a personal crisis which he had not foreseen or prepared for and which at the time he wholly failed to master. The story of that crisis—its slow growth and sudden breaking—is the main theme of the fifth and final section of this book.

Part 5

Casks for the Castaway

I dreamed, and behold, I saw a man, clothed in rags, stand-ing in a certain place, with his face from his own house, a book in his hand, and a great burden on his back. I looked, and saw him open the book, and read therein; and, as he read, he wept, and trembled; and, not being able longer to contain, he brake out with a lamentable cry, saying "What shall I do?" JOHN BUNYAN, *The Pilgrim's Progress*

Pip was at bottom very bright, with that pleasant, genial, jolly brightness peculiar to his tribe; a tribe, which ever en-joy all holidays and festivities with finer, freer relish than any other race . . . But Pip was left behind on the sea, like a hurried traveller's trunk.

HERMAN MELVILLE, *Moby Dick*

I

|||| Listening, hour after hour, week after week,
throughout seven months, to the words of a youth
undergoing trial for murder is a very different experience from reading an edited version of that boy's life—
even when the words are his own and page after page is
almost exact reproduction. For the reader, the context,
which gives the words their meaning, is missing.

A boy speaking; a man listening; a tape silently
recording. An air of detached, clinical sympathy per-
vading a quiet room. It sounds very peaceful, without
consequences or complications. It could hardly have
been more different. Outwardly, of course, our sessions
were peaceful enough; but they were far from being
innocent of consequence or free from complication. In
seven months a great deal can happen; it did. From the
very start, I profoundly affected Manuel's standing.
Reporters distracted him with attempts to interview
him or with short, wounding paragraphs in their papers.
Within two months of my visits, the prison authorities
could not guarantee his personal safety: he was transferred to the Detention Center downtown. He was
disturbed by the climate of violence in the jail and by
the two murders which occurred inside it. His family
quarreled with him. Judith, his girl, gave up seeing him.
The slow processes of his trial ground gradually to a
halt. Meanwhile, as the months of talking released
springs of hidden, hitherto unsuspected emotion within
him, his attitudes and the meaning he attached to our
meetings altered. Feelings long pent up burst their

banks, provoking personal crisis. As a result, his crime threatened to become what so far it had never been for him: a real part of his life, something for which he was morally responsible.

Some knowledge of this process and some insight into the background of his life within prison walls are essential to the understanding of Manuel's words.

I I

The early months until October were, for me at any rate, nerve-racking and exhausting. I passed into an unknown world. I was a forty-one-year-old, foreign, University professor; Manuel was a seventeen-year-old Chilean youth with a record of previous convictions, now on trial for one of the gravest crimes in the calendar. We faced each other, members of different tribes. I needed time to adjust myself to him; a breathing space to take stock of my new surroundings, to learn my way about. Manuel had no use for such luxuries as time at all. He dropped completely, though silently, the pretense that he was not the murderer; he gave me clearly and unmistakably to understand that of course he was. The need to pretend otherwise had given place to something far more imperious: the need to speak. Poor in all else, he was rich indeed in words.

Words. In front of prisoners, reporters, and representatives of official authority, he used them to brag, to strike a pose, to appear important. They were his substitute for the flashy clothes he no longer had. But once alone with me and sure that he had captured my full attention, he turned them to other, no less urgent uses. Almost they took possession of him. "An unceasing river," I called them in my diary; down these rapids he floated the frail raft of his life's story with a kind of grim desperation. He was trying, so it seemed to me, to make sense of his life, in some strange way to transform it, by casting the burden of it onto someone who would accept it and give it value. He had the concentrated determination and attitude of the Sunday painter for whom everything before his mind's eye deeply mattered; he did not stop speaking till he had pictured for me just as he had seen them all the flora and fauna that he encountered on his Mississippi journey through life. As self-absorbed as Bunyan, and possessed of the same belief in the infinite importance of small detail, he gave the impression that his own life was a mystery of the deepest and most urgent concern to him. Yet he was entirely unintrospective and totally innocent of the faintest curiosity in any other human being. He saw men as trees walking.

I was shocked by this. Normally, he never mentioned his immediate family at all. It was five months before I discovered that his Aunt Gloria had worked in a bar for sailors, or that Tía Anita's husband had been a cattle thief who had spent three years in jail and then deserted her. And then I only found out by chance. Manuel did not conceal these things from me: quite the contrary, they cropped up in conversation. He was surprised I did not know them. It was just that he was not interested in them. In all the months I knew Manuel, he cannot have spoken more than five minutes of his brother or his sister. He did not know what his brother's job was. Even his mother remained a dim figure in the background, like Orwell's Boxer recommending work as a solution to Manuel's problems or acting as a kind of ineffective chorus, chanting woe. He said she had once been pretty and that the scandal of his arrest for murder had aged her. He admitted that he had not got along with her. Nothing more. His comments about his stepfather summed up his attitude toward them all: he did not avoid them, it was just that their paths never crossed. He never thought of them at all.

Curiously enough, even his attitude towards his father changed when I brought the subject up again several months later. I asked him what he remembered of him and why as a child he had cared more for his father than for his mother. He remembered he had attended his father's funeral, but nothing else. And he added, most matter-of-factly, almost with indifference, that he supposed he had liked his father more because he had beaten him less. Gone was the sharp contrast between his parents; they were now on a sliding scale.

Tía Berta, the aunt who took care of him since the age of five, is another story. She was most important to him and affected his life profoundly. In my diary I described what seemed to me to be his attitude to her and his uncle in these words: "Manuel's Aunt Berta, who is quite the most important figure in this part of his story (*i.e.*, his account of his life up to the age of fifteen) emerges as the principal representative of authority in his life and as a shrewd, energetic woman of business. But what she was like as a woman can only be guessed from scraps and fragments gleaned from Manuel's talk on other matters, and from what he records her as doing. She was nearly twenty years older than his mother; and she much preferred Jaime, who was lame, to his younger brother. He saw her as a tireless, extremely active woman, preoccupied with business. . . . She was capable, apparently, of extraordinary forms of relaxation, and when her heart was touched, she could be both generous and unwise. Yet in Manuel's incurious, unloving eyes she appeared only as his chief antagonist; powerful, shrewd at times, but mainly indifferent in a battle he waged, sometimes with one weapon, sometimes with another, to secure two main objectives—escape from the apartment into the street, and the status conferred by clothes. Indeed, his description of this woman in love with a workman of whom she was jealous was as uncomprehending and bizarre as the twelve-year-old Leo Colston's vision of Marian Maudsley in Hartley's *The Go-Between,* and a good deal more heartless. Though Manuel was by no means so innocent as Leo, he appeared similarly as a tool of his aunt's self-interested schemes. The difference was that Manuel was astute enough to make use of her, too.

"As a representative of authority, she was intensely self-absorbed, anxious not to be bothered, content with issuing prohibitions which she was either too busy or too indifferent to see enforced, very tolerant of grave violations of trust within the family, but instant to punish breaches that occurred outside it which threatened to bring the family into disrepute. An authority that was venal and fraudulent, she did not hesitate to make deals that were casually and conveniently broken when her immediate purpose was secured; and she was hard to persuade to meet her admitted obligations. A living symbol, in fact, of what to disenchanted adult eyes is a Chilean government department. To Manuel, however, she appeared rather as a force of nature: to be observed, respected, predicted, circumvented, and controlled. Again and again I tried to provoke him into an expression of feeling or a moral judgment on the loveless indifference of her behavior towards him. It was useless: the penny never dropped. It was not that he was held back by loyalty, that strongest of Chilean moral sentiments; it was just that as a person she did not exist. Such was Huck's vision of his father.

"Manuel spoke of his aunt with the respect due to a dynamic force of nature; for his uncle he felt only contempt. Feckless, lazy, and irresponsible, this uninteresting nonentity hung up his hat for good in his aunt's house. As a person, he made no impact on Manuel whatsoever: they seem to have viewed each other, like fellow lodgers in a flophouse, with perfect indifference."

As a comment on the character of Manuel's aunt, these notes are of course harsh and one-sided. Later in his story, Manuel's attitude toward her changed. Tía Berta may have been—indeed, she clearly was—in-

different to him; she found him a nuisance and ended
by regarding him as a pest. She tried to rid herself of
him first by putting him in institutions and later by
expelling him from her home. Her motive was also
family pride, never affection; her reaction to his arrest
for murder was thankfulness that she had washed her
hands of him at the age of fifteen, marked unwillingness
to make any declaration in court concerning him, and
fear that her name would appear in the papers as a
murderer's aunt and that she would be recognized in
the streets by strangers. She almost never visited him
when he was in jail, and desired only to be left in peace.
All this is true. But there is a good deal that can be said
in her favor. She voluntarily accepted full responsibility
for her brother's three children. She clothed, fed, sheltered, and educated them for more than twenty years;
Manuel's elder brother Jaime continued his education
up to the sixth year of secondary school, married and
brought his wife to live with him in his aunt's house; his
sister Lucía is still living there. Tía Berta may have
shunted Manuel off to boarding school at the tender age
of eight, but she brought him home again when his
truancy ceased. Only he of the three children turned
out badly. So far as I know, neither Jaime nor Lucía
ever got into trouble with the police. That Berta ended
by feeling only resentment toward Manuel can hardly
be held against her. The wonder is that she did not feel
more. Nor were her comments about him as a boy
unkindly. She remembered him as mild-mannered and
respectful, almost passive. He puzzled her by roaming

the streets for long hours at night; he never raised a hand against her. Though she rarely visited him now, even Manuel recognized that the money his mother used to buy the food and clothes that kept him in prison came from her. Again, Manuel did later judge her as a person. He considered her as hostile and unfriendly, but willing ultimately to provide for him. A bleak, correct judgment, only less harsh than that he adopted toward his uncle. For him, his contempt and dislike never wavered. It may have been deserved.

Even at the end of seven months, when Manuel's capacity for feeling had returned to him, he remained to an astonishing degree affectionless. And in these early months he exhibited an extreme withdrawal from human feeling.

This lack of feeling was brought home to me in another way; by his attitude to violence. Roberto, the student who had originally invited me to visit the jail, frequently used to come with me when I saw the boys, and they had got to know and like him. About a month or so after he had entered the prison with me for the first time, Roberto and his brother were "coshed" while returning home in the early hours of the morning from a party in the center of town, and badly beaten up. The attack was quite unprovoked and pointless, their assailants had not robbed them—they had simply run away.

When the boys came to hear of this, they were indignant on Roberto's behalf (not, of course, on his brother's; he was an officer in the prison). They made a point of sympathizing with him and offered to exact dire retribution upon the offenders. (In this they were doomed to disappointment. One of the two men was caught, but he had money, friends, and a private lawyer. He spent eight days in the Detention Center and was then set free.)

Not so Garcés. Never once did he so much as mention Roberto's misfortune. His awareness of the attack took another form; it served to stimulate a flood of memories of acts of violence in which he had taken part. My diary notes, written a week after my visit to him, comment as follows:

"Due to the attack on Roberto, I saw Garcés a day later than I had intended. Would he make any mention of the event? I was curious to see. My strong guess was that he would not; he was too self-absorbed. Throughout the two hours and a half in which we were alone, he gave no hint concerning it. Overtly, at least; but the material we covered together in our private session dealt almost entirely with the armed robbery, gang murder, beatings, and escapes into hiding in which he had been directly or indirectly involved. Was this material prompted by Garcés' knowledge of what had just happened? Was he competing and comparing himself, unconsciously, with those assailants, or was he just capping one story with a number of others describing equally pitiless and pointless crimes? As usual, in his long account of these things there was no hint of any human sympathy for anyone; and, as usual, with the single exception of his girl—no one received a name. Not the boy with whom he held up a crowded café one midnight at pistol point (though the pistol had only blanks), nor the boy in whose house he hid from the police, nor the woman with whom he stayed for four days when he was turned out of his aunt's house at the age of fifteen. Again, I could feel—it was almost palpable—the pressure of his need to talk, to tell his story, all his story, before it was too late; he seemed to fear that something might happen to interrupt it. Perhaps that he would be transferred to the adults' section and no longer be able to see me, or that I might weary of him and transfer my attention and interest to someone else. There was the same desire to tell me everything, but that day his sense of time seemed particularly confused. He showed the same dislike of interruption, always returning with barely concealed impatience to the point in his narrative at which he had been cut short.

"In the midst of his story the electric light failed. We were plunged into the dark. He asked for a match; I did not have one. We sat on, invisible to each other, talking for a full twenty minutes. I felt vaguely uneasy—thus must Mercier have been in his office on that fateful evening in May. But I ignored this; what else could I do? Garcés proceeded serenely with his horrifying narrative of armed robbery and gang warfare, far too interested in his own story to bother about the lights.

"It was still raining when I rose to go. I collected my belongings—my briefcase, umbrella, the odd paraphernalia incidental to a trip to the jail. I struggled rather inefficiently into my mackintosh. Garcés stood silent, watching. He did not offer to help."

Of course he did not: he no more thought of me as a person than a penitent does his invisible confessor in church. I was his lifeline, his trumpet to the outside world, his defense against it, his psychiatrist, his priest: a necessary presence, but emphatically not a friend. Manuel was talking to himself.

His image of himself was a confused one. As a slum child, he had early been transferred from this environment to the "respectable" world of the lower middle class, if only to the bottom rung of it. He had not been able to stay there. Pitchforked into private boarding schools for the poor, the uncared-for, and the ill-treated, he had developed many of the characteristics of the institutional child; at fifteen and a half, he was back again in the adobe-house atmosphere from which he had been rescued ten years earlier. In a sense, this was his native air, but he was not now at home there. He had acquired in the meantime many of his aunt's standards of judgment: in particular, he saw his mother and her family through Berta's eyes, as responsible for his father's death and as low and undesirable. He had also an education which had lasted at least three, if not four, years longer than that of most boys of his class; he had a much greater command of language than the average; he disliked foul language, at least in others, and did not swear. It was typical of him that one of his main charges against his uncle was that he coarsened his aunt and made her foulmouthed. It was also like him to describe a friend like López as "different from the other boys" and to remember two years after the event a simi-

lar compliment paid him by a tart in bed. These were
judgments of manners: he meant "more refined and
better class." In fact, both Carlos López and Arancibia
the tailor were a cut above the run-of-the-mill poor thief.
López was better mannered than most of the other
boys, looked cleaner and more decent; he gave the impression of being a gay, irresponsible, attractive schoolboy of seventeen. Arancibia, who was twenty-three, was
even more strikingly respectable in appearance, and
much more intelligent than the average prisoner. He
was granted special privileges and lived among the
small minority of good-conduct and well-to-do prisoners
on the first floor. He was a dapper young man, short,
clean, neatly dressed, with a small, well-trimmed beard,
a clever, sensitive, bad-tempered face, and big, keen
eyes. I should have guessed he was a radio mechanic
with a taste for classical music; he gave the impression
of being enterprising, artistic, and self-educated. In
fact, he was all these things. He fancied himself also
as a singer; I met him because he wanted me to record
his voice.

This uncertainty of status came out also, in part at
least, in Manuel's extreme touchiness and lack of humor
and in his refusal to accept direction or advice from
anyone. This was particularly evident in his attitudes
toward the lawyers who represented him at different
times. One lawyer dropped out almost at once. Manuel
said the lawyer gave him a lot of advice about what to
say, which he took no notice of—a reaction highly
reminiscent of his response to the detective's advice two

years earlier. The second lawyer, who like the first was a private one, was dry, abrupt in manner, and business-like. Manuel professed at first to approve of this; he added unenthusiastically that he liked the man because he brought cigarettes and magazines when he called. He did not, however, regard the lawyer's actions as disinterested, and commented that he was proposing to charge four hundred escudos for his services, plus traveling expenses. Later, Manuel was to qualify this more severely still; the lawyer had offended him by addressing him without preliminary in the familiar *tú*. He had no liking for him at all, he now admitted. The state lawyer, a woman who came in the end to take charge of his case, he did not trust. He extended to her the same treatment he had originally shown me: he adopted an attitude of lofty self-satisfaction. She found him disconcerting; he, on his side, seemed unwilling to receive help.

Long before he illustrated these characteristics for me in his story or told me of his reactions to his lawyers, I felt their presence. I was always most careful never to seem to patronize, always to accept information from him modestly, never—never, under any circumstances —to offer advice. From the start I asked him whether he wished me to address him in the familiar or the formal mode; I received permission to use *tú*. I never tried to lead him. At the slightest hint of authority, he bridled. Within this framework, however, he was highly co-operative and most respectful. Never, at any time, did we clash.

Most of all, perhaps, his uncertainty showed itself in an obsessive concern with clothes. Of course, most young men everywhere worry over their clothes when they first go out on a date; most schoolboys learn to judge class, and judge it pretty accurately, by a swift, appraising glance at a shirt or a pair of shoes. A boy's battles to secure new clothing or his tears of joy at Christmas must be common enough occurrences in a hundred homes; poor children are inured to living in a world of beatings and promised watches. But Manuel's concern went far beyond this.

Chile's poor are not, on the whole, especially clothes-conscious; a working-class man does not make a point of dressing up on Sunday, nor does he feel ashamed to be seen in the streets in his working clothes. For one thing, he cannot afford to feel otherwise. Suits are too expensive. For another, a concern with clothes as a token of status is, in Chile, a middle-class habit, nowhere more cruel or obsessive than among the young. A working-class youth does not normally feel the need to compete with his peers on that battlefield. Manuel did. Just because his status in his own home and outside it was so uncertain, he did feel the need continually to assert his claims. But he had no weapons to enforce them.

Time and again, he staked a claim among his fellows not only to personal worth but to middle-class status; time and again, those claims were rejected. Every threat to his pride he saw in terms of dress; he parried them all with appeals to fashion. Always, the surest index of

Manuel's self-judgment occurs, in his story, when he looks himself up and down and pronounces sentence. In the grocer's, when he is being insulted; in the graveyard, when Silvia is passing by; on the run before his murder; even, when arrested, "How do I look?" was the one important question.

He thought of himself as a habitual thief; the first part of his story was designed to show how he became one. In our very first session, the episode of the theft of the teacher's money, with its aftermath, was his climax; everything in his story led up to it. He was not ashamed of thieving. It was simply a habit by which he had also from time to time made his living. A habit, but not a regular occupation. He had started stealing to compensate for loss, and to get back at people—his teacher, his aunt, his uncle—for their treatment of him. Later, through chance contacts in the plaza, he drifted into the habit of stealing to obtain what he wanted with a minimum of effort. Robbery with violence he went in for as much for fun as for money; in the end, it became merely a means of making money in temporary difficulties. He felt no sense of guilt. In those early months he did not think of himself as a professional criminal.

He accepted the fact that he was a murderer, but purely externally. He was a murderer by accident, and he was not proud of the fact. Of course, he exploited the fact inside the jail to obtain prestige, but that maneuver was purely tactical. In this, as in other matters, his feelings were also to change. In the early months his reputation as a murderer was a bare fact which might prove useful in his fight for recognition inside the jail.

His attitude toward his trial throughout these months was most curious. To start with, he was exceedingly ignorant concerning the whole process. This was by no means his own fault. Chilean trials do not take place in a public setting, before judge and counsel and jury, in the presence of the accused. They proceed bureaucratically. Declarations are taken; documents filed; witnesses are confronted. The defense lawyer submits further documents and finally a written defense. When all the documents are in, the judge reads them in the privacy of his study and in due course pronounces sentence. Even the sentence is only another document, which is later to be handed to the accused. Most prisoners who are poor have only the dimmest conception of what is going on.

Manuel, however, was doubly in darkness. He told me grandly that he was quite conversant with the documents of his trial, was well aware of what was happening, and had a private lawyer representing him. On all these points he was completely mistaken. He had no idea whatever of the strength of the case against him; he had read only his own statements and was firmly convinced that they were the only solid evidence of his guilt; he had no notion at all of the court's procedures. He had complained in front of the boys that he had seen his lawyer "all too often." In fact, he was referring to the number of times he had appeared in court to testify. His lawyer was never present. By Chilean law, he was not even permitted to be. Neither did he have a private lawyer. For whatever reason, the two men who had at the beginning of the case offered to take him on had since dropped out; it was left to the state to provide him with counsel. Nor did he have any idea what his sentence was likely to be: at different times he would assess it at a year and a half, five years; once he ventured on ten.

The whole thing was quite unreal to him; throughout September and October he hardly once referred to it. Even the boys noticed this with surprise and commented on the fact both to him and to me. Santos, who liked to carry tales, reported that after one session with me, Garcés had complained that I had made him work his brain too hard, considering he had his trial to worry about. Santos's rejoinder was interesting. "You!" he said, in tones of withering scorn, "you never worry about your trial at all; you hardly give it a thought!" Then, turning to me, he added: "It's true, you know; Garcés spends whole days without ever thinking about it." I could believe him.

As for his crime, he was in considerable confusion about the attitude to adopt to it. After he had taken back his retraction, he was still telling both reporters and the boys in the jail that he was not guilty; yet in public he seemed most anxious to claim the credit for his crime. In private, with me, he began by denying his guilt and producing a newspaper report to confirm what he was saying; a few weeks later he dropped all this and

proceeded always on the assumption that he had committed the crime. For a brief period he used terms like
"this business" to refer to the murder; he soon gave
them up in favor of the ordinary terms of common
speech—kill, murder, murderer. He even taught me
with a touch of conscious pride the legal terms in
Spanish. He spoke without fuss or shame; it was he who
put me at ease, not I him. He was quite confident that
he would be able to give me a full and truthful account
of his crime. He had done it before; he could do it again.
Anyway, it was all down in the documents. He spoke of
the whole matter entirely without emotion or embarrassment. There was no doubt that at the time he was
perfectly sincere. He had also forgotten that less than
six weeks earlier he had told me that he had not done
it.

III

My dealings with Manuel were not confined to our
private sessions. I saw him also as a member of the
menores group, when—in theory—he sank into the
background to take his chances along with the rest. Of
course, it was not like that at all.

He had failed to gain the respect of his fellows with
his crime. Now he was to try his luck exploiting his
connection with me. In this new tactic he was moder-
ately successful. Whenever, for instance, I would appear
in the prison yard or in the corridors of the compound,
he would show up from nowhere and try to act as my

sole escort. He would seek to appropriate me in public; he gained kudos by introducing me to Arancibia, the tailor with whom he worked. He was also helped by a change in the composition of the *menores* group. Within quite a short time of my arrival, six of the original fifteen left the group, including three of the toughs—two of them on bail, paid for by me, the third to join the adult section. Their places were taken soon enough by others, but the character of the group was no longer the same. In particular, the toughs were left without a natural leader. Rather surprisingly, they made use of Garcés intermittently to represent their cause. This brought him into collision with Santos, the acknowledged leader. As a result, my difficulties in helping the boys as a whole were markedly increased. Manuel's jealousy of Santos, however, gave him some fellow feeling for him. He had never been a leader before; he was hardly one now; but at least he was competing with a leader, which was a good deal better than being nowhere at all.

In other ways, Manuel lost out. Due to his rivalry with the official leader, he did not get his fair share of the things I brought; and I could not step in to protect him. After my arrival too, the prison authorities made an effort to implement the official theory—that boys and men were to be kept in separate parts of the prison during the daytime—by banishing the boys to an isolated yard. When this happened, Manuel at once lost his rights in the tailor's cell. He could no longer work or eat with him. The separation never became rigid, and in the following weeks, more or less provisionally and *sub rosa,* Manuel gravitated back into the tailor's orbit. But the precarious arrangement was always liable to sudden change.

Manuel was in any case gradually losing his foothold there. The two men quarreled regularly; Manuel, as regularly, cried. Arancibia, who was reported to be very hot-tempered and jealous, was always threatening to expel him from the cell. There was also every chance that the tailor would be leaving the prison shortly on conditional discharge. Manuel was in danger of losing his protection. Partly perhaps to remedy this growing sense of insecurity, and to gain a reputation for manliness, he went in for the drugs that were circulating in the prison and got drunk on spirit alcohol. The only effect of this was that he wound up in the prison sickroom with a bad throat. In the eyes of his fellows he remained Susie.

Then, suddenly, at the beginning of October he did something for which everyone was unprepared. He went off one evening to the courts, apparently to make some further statement in his trial; he returned having brought charges against three prisoners for rape and extortion. These were three toughs. One was the eighteen-year-old who had been transferred to the adult section; the second was a minor still in the minors' group; and the third was a boy whose bail I had paid and who had since absconded. Manuel again became incommunicado, but the response to his unheard-of action was instant. As it was immediately and automatically assumed that Arancibia was behind the move, three men entered his cell next day while he was working and stabbed him. Manuel, incommunicado, was temporarily safe; but ways were found to threaten him. When his term of isolation was at an end, he was therefore transferred for his own protection to the Detention Center downtown. The prison itself had no means of protecting him.

Again reporters came; his name reappeared in the papers. This did him no good and won him no sympathy. His family was mortified by the renewed publicity; the accused boys exploited the fact to claim that Manuel had brought the charge in order to keep himself in the news; and his action served notice to the prison population at large, if they had not already suspected it, that Manuel was now "available."

It took me about two weeks to get in touch with him in the Detention Center, and I chose the date of his eighteenth birthday—October 19—to make my appearance. I remember the occasion very well. I was waiting for him in the yard when I saw him walking toward me with that air of suppressed truculence that he always adopted toward official authority. When he caught sight of me his face changed completely; it shone with pleasure, wreathed in smiles. He was not just pleased, he was delighted to see me. I congratulated him on his birthday and gave him my present—a shirt, tie, and pullover. Since he had lost all his possessions while he was incommunicado, he was badly in need of them. I could see he was pleased to receive a present, but he was also disappointed at what I had brought. They did not suit his taste; they were too sober. We began again.

He referred to the events unleashed by his charges against the boys as "my latest adventures," but he was not anxious to discuss them, saying he preferred to wait till he reached the appropriate point in his story to tell of them. Very much in character, of course. However, on this occasion I pressed him. The rape occurred three weeks after he had arrived in the prison, when the fear the boys felt towards a self-confessed murderer had worn off and they had come to see him as one of them, but weaker. After taking advantage of him one night in his cell, they had threatened to betray him to his family and "sell" him to the men. He had preferred to pay up. In the end, the price had become too heavy. After a considerable effort, he had taken his courage in both hands and denounced them to the court. Arancibia had had nothing whatever to do with it. Manuel surprised me greatly at this interview by treating me for the first time as a person and addressing me with a directness he had not previously shown. It was not just that I had come in search of him in his new prison, or that I had remembered his birthday; he had decided he liked me. This was quite new.

Our relations changed. His circumstances in the Detention Center had a great deal to do with this. Manuel has himself described life in the Center; there is no reason for me to add much to what he said. It was considerably cleaner, more comfortable, and more civilized for most of its inhabitants than the jail. It had a large floating population. Many were not professional criminals at all, and a proportion were respectable, decent men unfortunate enough to be obliged to spend a routine four days in the Center because they were thought to be connected, if only as witnesses, with some crime. There were no roaming gangs of tough criminals, and the place did not give the impression of a slum. It was a sort of cross between an army depot and a vast railway waiting room: everyone was on the way somewhere—either back to liberty or on to jail. The Center was also much more accessible to outside influences. It was in the middle of town; visitors were very frequent; the yard where the detained met and talked with their families had park benches and was by no means disagreeable or oppressive to sit in.

For Manuel, in particular, it offered many advantages. He was now, officially, an adult; he slept in a large, thirty-bunk dormitory in which (at first) no one pestered him. He was free to wander about, without danger of assault, and choose his friends. For two and a half months he was not unhappy. The accident of his transfer also carried with it other quite unforeseen benefits. Of these the biggest was that he no longer had to compete with the other boys for my attention, as he now had me to himself, and I no longer had to strike a balance between their claims and his. I could mark his birthday or do him favors without having to weigh the consequences; I was free to attend undistracted to his personal needs. This, coupled with the fact that, far from leaving him to his fate, I had gone in search of him

to continue our meetings, had momentous consequences. He ceased to be anxious that I might lose
interest in him and give up coming; he noticeably
relaxed in our sessions; he chatted comfortably after
them; he even swallowed his pride on occasion to admit
that he was in need and to ask me for a favor.

He asked for the minimum and never tried to exploit
me. He began to enjoy our meetings as a form of
relaxation and society. He would tell me in an expansive
mood that he was writing poems or reading books; we
would exchange notes about films. He took these things
seriously, even pretentiously, and would treat the por-
nography that was circulating in the Center with the
same solemnity as the Chilean novels that he had read
in snippets in the classroom and pretended he had read
entire. He was bored in the Center and asked me to
come more frequently.

Indeed, throughout November and December there
were notable changes. Like a boy at a boarding school
for whom the routine of term time provides a sense of
needed security, he adapted himself to the rhythm of
life in the Center, which he did not find uncongenial.
He gravitated naturally toward the young men of his
age and class who were thieves or accused of murder;
he adopted, insensibly, the standard thieves' code; he
recited as an article of faith, and blindly believed it, that
ponces and exploiters of women were worse than other
criminals and that society was to blame for crime. He
was coming to think of himself as a criminal. (This was

the period in which he described his early life in jail.)

About his trial he continued to think hardly at all. His lawyer had explained his defense to him; he knew he was due for psychiatric examination. He was really not particularly interested. When the date came for the interview itself, outside the prison, his only anxiety was clothes, and he asked me to take a message to his aunt's house in which he appealed to his brother for the loan of some. His comment, after the examination, was that it had proved negative. "I wasn't mad," he said. At this time I started checking up on his story. I went round to the schools he had been at and talked to the nuns and the teachers; I tracked down his mother's adobe house on a distant hill and his aunt's house five minutes from the Detention Center; Manuel asked me to meet his mother. I read all the documents of the trial, spoke with his lawyer, and met, accidentally and in another setting, one of the psychiatrists selected by the court to examine him. I kept him informed of what I was doing and told him how I proposed to write my book. He was keenly interested. Interested, and very proud. He told his lawyer, and let it be known inside the jail, that there was a gentleman engaged in writing his biography. He enjoyed the idea of my playing Boswell to his Johnson.

My conversations with the nuns fully vindicated Manuel's claim to almost total recall. The picture he gave of places and routines which here I have only sketched was materially accurate down to the smallest

detail. Of course his child's vision of events was different
from that of elderly nuns. In particular, the account of
the theft that led to his removal from the first school was
not correct in its details. A nun who had been there
more than fifteen years, a kindly and cheerful woman
well over sixty, remembered the incident well. Manuel,
whom she described as a dark, plump little boy, had not
taken a thousand pesos—he had taken the teacher's
whole monthly salary. He had not been expelled; he
had been removed by his aunt. And she had acted in
indignation, protesting that her nephew would never
have done such a thing—though the nephew, as the nun
remarked, had admitted the theft. The school had only
asked the aunt to pay the money back: she had refused
and taken away the child.

The nun in the second school also remembered him.
She was still a young woman, and a very pretty one; she
said he had been particularly well-behaved. Then she
laughed and said it was a pity, because she remembered
best the boys who gave most trouble. Both schools were
homes for very poor, virtually abandoned children. The
buildings inside and out were very clean, light, and in
good condition. Physically they were in far better shape
than either the Casa de Menores, the State Remand
Home, or the Refugio de Cristo, a privately supported
home for abandoned children, run by priests. The
children were also kept a good deal busier. In fact,
apart from their school classes, they seemed in the
second school very regimented indeed. They attended
Mass at seven every morning, said the Rosary every

evening; learned Latin or singing; spent a good deal of time cleaning the building and had less than an hour a day free for play. The school had about fifty boys in it; there were also a few babies. Perhaps the best comment on the feelings of the children in these homes was the presence of a stucco statue of a saint, placed in the corner of the playground, to whom they prayed that someone from outside might come to visit them. Neither of the two nuns who remembered Manuel had any idea what had become of him.

I V

This happy state of affairs could not last; by the beginning of January it was already coming to an end. There were all sorts of warning signals. To start with, Manuel lost ground among the prisoners in the Detention Center. Ever since he had been transferred from the jail, his work had ceased and he was dependent on his family for food. At first his mother provided it. Then she began to falter. There would be days when she couldn't or wouldn't come, and Manuel would have nothing to eat but what others could give him. When he appealed to me I helped him over the crisis; but he was chary of asking me often, and I suspect he was sometimes in a jam. Meanwhile, the case against the three boys lagged for lack of solid evidence, and the men in the Center began making public advances toward Manuel which he did not reject with sufficient energy. Worse still, the Gamonal family and Judith in particular were falling by the wayside. It was inevitable but it hurt him, though he said little about it. He also became very sensitive to press publicity. No wonder. Both his family and the court, for different reasons, had objected to his granting interviews to reporters, which had been taped and broadcast on local networks. Even he, acutely sensitive to ridicule as he was, and always on the lookout for fear of being laughed at inside the jail—even he could see that the comment was mocking and hostile, that it destroyed his reputation inside the prison instead of enhancing it, and he deeply resented it. He told me the reporters had treated him with mock servility, like a schoolchild, offering him sweets in return for an interview; yet he had not refused them. And he always feared a reference in the press to his missing fingers.

It became daily more evident that the carapace of unfeeling insouciance which had hitherto shielded him from any awareness of his situation was wearing thin. From mid-December, as I listened to him, I could see evidence of his growing capacity to feel again. A man died in his cell suddenly of a heart attack one midnight in the bunk next to him. He was an old man, in his sixties, and had spent most of his life in and out of jail. His son had owned or managed a bar in the dock area in which Manuel's aunt had worked. The sight of his death moved Manuel; he felt sorry for him, and he later suffered nightmares. At night prisoners ran berserk in the Center, had fights, suffered delusions of grandeur. Manuel professed to find this funny, a welcome diversion, a matter for laughter, but it got him down and he could not sleep. Even in the books he read, smut though some of them were, he became sensitive to the suffering of the characters, particularly of women.

Sometimes we talked of sex. In August and September he had spoken of the two nights he had spent with Silvia—briefly, but quite without embarrassment and certainly without emotion. This was his first experience with a woman, and he was proud of it. Whether it was pleasurable he did not say. He described next and more briefly his night with Susana. This he admitted under questioning he did not enjoy. It was still important to him: it was the third time he had been to bed with a woman. He was only fifteen; a matter for pride. In the Detention Center in November he became more expansive. When I asked him if he had enjoyed his night with the anonymous girl in the hotel bedroom, he thought for a moment and replied: "She had a very pretty body. Yes, I did." It was not a very eloquent or enthusiastic testimonial.

A month or two later I asked him to tell me something of his sexual development. He looked sad and fell silent. "It's all very disagreeable," he said. "I'd prefer to think of something pleasanter." I did not press him. But this was his settled attitude. As for his relations with men, he answered my questions with extreme brevity and marked distaste. The memory of the occasions disgusted him; he insisted that his experiences were limited to the three he had mentioned. Manuel was coming alive again. Most of all, he was becoming aware of his situation. All the documents were now in; his trial had ended; he had only to await indefinitely his sentence. He tried not to face this reality at all. In a unique moment of self-knowledge, or self-criticism, he confessed to me: "I am trying to forget where I am." He was not succeeding.

V

As in his story he drew gradually nearer the date of his crime, he contracted a throat ailment which prevented him from speaking. He evinced an unaccountable reluctance to complete and hand in the notebook I had given him in which to supplement the recorded story. Twice he did something which for him was unheard of: he sent word to say that he was too busy to keep his appointment. He dallied in his story, spinning out episodes, marking time. This period also coincided, as luck would have it, with no less than three murders—two in the jail, one in town. Manuel knew most of the people connected with them. He knew the victim of the first jail murder—a leader of one of the gangs that specialized in assaulting boys. In the town case, he had met the murderer—a fourteen-year-old boy, a prostitute's son, who had been accused of killing his twenty-three-year-old lover. Manuel had the opportunity of renewing his acquaintance with this boy in the Detention Center.

Though he could chat coolly of these matters, he was now controlling a new and hitherto unsuspected emotion. I became more and more convinced that he would never be able to bring himself to go over the events of his crime again. In fact, I doubted very much whether I even had the right to ask him to do so. I suggested he might, if he preferred, just skip it. He neither accepted nor rejected my offer.

Over the last two months, as a matter of fact, he had supplied me with a good deal of incidental information concerning the murder. I had spent many hours reading his enormous file in one of the offices of the courtroom, had jotted down the questions I wanted to ask him, and after our sessions with the recorder I would talk to him of the work I had done. Then I would raise my queries. His behavior was quite unlike what he had so confidently predicted it would be. His fantastic, photographic memory still operated, as ever, with all its old efficiency, but he wished to discuss his crime as little as he had cared earlier to speak of sex. For the same reason: he was horrified and disgusted by it.

It was not just that he had not meant to kill the lawyer; at no time had it ever entered his head that he might possibly have done so. Even when the papers had been full of it and the radio was blaring it forth, Manuel was absolutely certain that it was not true. He had read thrillers in which the police try to catch a thief by pretending that his victim is dead. He remained firmly convinced that the newspaper ballyhoo was a police stunt. It was not till his arrest that he realized Mercier was really and truly dead.

In the light of this, most of the other things he told me made good sense. He knew of course that the police were out looking for him. They had been searching for him, as he pointed out to me, since the end of March, but they had not found him. Nor did he see any reason why they should catch him now. He had no sense of danger. Even in retrospect, he saw nothing foolhardy about returning to the Cachás Grandes Café and rubbing shoulders with the police. He was often there when they were looking for him; he thought it was the safest place to be. In April he had even met López' brother, the policeman, there, without ill result. The police had a drawing of him based on the descriptions of witnesses; they still failed to see him.

Besides, he thought of himself as a thief, not a murderer. "A thief never thinks he'll be caught. Ask any of 'em." Indeed, his behavior in May chimed in well with the standard pattern of his behavior after a robbery. He had always been careless and unconcerned to hide his tracks. He did not get rid of Mercier's wallet and identity cards, for instance, because he thought he would always have time to do so, if need arose. He had cashed the forged check in a shop where he was known—precisely for that reason, because it would be accepted without question. He had known that it would be questioned; he just did not consider the consequences. He resented the suggestion that he had gone around showing to all and sundry the wallet and checkbooks he had stolen, but he was quite ready to admit that they might have been seen by anyone when he emptied his pockets. He had always acted thus. For Manuel, his encounter with Mercier was the last of a series of robberies and acts of violence which began after he left the Gamonal family with only one escudo in his pocket and no chance of making any money by honest means.

He looked back on that month with pain and considerable humiliation. He made no bones about the fact that he had gone out every evening, sometimes alone, sometimes in company, to rob. He stole whatever he could lay hands on—radios, car lights, the glass from the windows of coaches or trains; he sold what he could to fences. Defrauded of success in these endeavors, he would roam the streets as a footpad, waylaying and assaulting drunks. He squandered his money, fell into debt to fences, went on jags. He spent the night in cheap hotel bedrooms or in brothels; sometimes, when drunk, he slept it off on beaches; twice arrested on suspicion, he passed the night in jail.

His morale was failing; he felt desperate; he sank into self-disgust. A sure sign of this was his own admission that he became daily less presentable; he grew so dark and grimy that he felt even his family would not recognize him. He lost touch with the Gamonal family; he was ashamed to visit them. This was the context in which he placed his sexual encounters with men. He made no excuses, pretended no ignorance. He needed money. He resented and disliked the men.

When it came to speaking of Mercier, he was emphatic that the lawyer had strung him along with promises of work and money, giving him nothing; the sexual act filled him with "very great disgust." He repeated, anxiously, that he had only meant to threaten and would have been quite satisfied to have come away with five escudos in his pocket. I raised the obvious objections to this statement of motive. He listened, looked down sadly, crumpled. I thought he was going to cry. "I really don't know why I went there; I don't know why I did it." It was the literal truth.

The old Manuel reasserted himself when he came to speak of his arrest. It was the things that hurt his pride—the handcuffs, the humiliating treatment—that he remembered with most bitterness. He would not have been true to himself if he had not mentioned as the crowning insult that his hair had been pulled down so hard over his face in the questioning that it would not go back into place when the reporters came to the station to take his photograph. Manuel was not sorry for what he had done. He was appalled by it. This was a deeper, more primitive, and much more violent emotion than a moral one; it was also entirely different. His act appalled him because it was completely unintended and unexpected by him. But the action he had intended was, for Manuel, within the range of the permissible. Not, precisely, the morally permissible; he did not see robbery or violence in moral terms at all, any more than a smuggler or a reckless driver stops to consider his activities in these terms. It was a way of making money in difficult circumstances. In this exceptional instance, he had struck far harder than he had ever intended, though he did not know why; and this he very much regretted. Of theft itself, however, he did not feel guilty. If you got away with it, well and good; if not, you paid for it dearly enough in prison. Jail wiped the slate clean; society was quits. It was as simple as that. His was the morality of the mouse with the cat.

He could not face the fact that he had committed murder. He could use his crime to attempt to achieve status in jail, but he was not proud of it. On the contrary, its enormity overwhelmed him, and he tried to dodge the reality by concentrating on the details. I began to see why his confessions read so like descriptions written by the latest French novelists; he adopted the same technique of emotional evasion. By atomizing the account of his acts, he destroyed their reality. The result was to make his crime appear senseless, the criminal a monster. In fact, he was hiding from himself.

All this I gathered, casually, at different times, after sessions in December and early January. Then, suddenly, just before I was due to leave the city for three weeks, Manuel reached in a single burst the period of his crime. He had raced to arrive there during the session, like a man who had been holding back for a long time from the sea's edge but had resolved at last to make the plunge. But once he had reached this point he stopped suddenly, at once surprised and upset. "I must stop and think about the next part," he said. "It's all a muddle in my mind. I committed so many robberies in those weeks that I've got them all mixed up. I must first write them down."

I turned the tape recorder off at once. As we still had nearly an hour ahead of us, I asked him if he would like to think aloud. But he was unbudgeable—he wanted to

order his thoughts on paper first. This suggestion, which
sounds so sensible, was in fact quite farcically out of
character. I had often urged Manuel to write his story
down, or produce pen pictures of his family, or keep a
diary of his days in jail; I was perpetually providing him
with a new pen or notebook to help him to do so. Quite
in vain: they were always being lost or lent or made the
victims of strange, implausible misadventures. No, he
was clearly baulking. It was not hard to guess at
what.

I accepted his decision philosophically and reminded
him that in any case he would have plenty of time, as I
would not be back to see him for nearly a month. We
could pick up again when I returned.

V I

On my return in late February I went to see Manuel
again. I was waiting for him as usual in the courtyard of
the Detention Center when I caught sight of him on his
way. He came toward me quickly, on his guard, determined, unfriendly—just as he had when I had gone in
search of him on his birthday four months earlier. I
looked forward now to seeing his smile of recognition.
Usually he would shake hands with me and walk
forward eagerly into the small office we used for our
meetings together, anxious to waste no time before
getting down to business. Today he greeted me coldly.
There was no need for me to stay, he told me outright.
We should not meet again.

I was, stupidly, hurt by this dismissal; I was even more astonished. But he was well within his rights, and this I admitted instantly. I only asked him to tell me why he was exercising them. It was only then, and still with great reluctance, that he consented to enter the office to talk to me. It was a shabby room, stuffy, drab and dark, squeezed underneath a staircase which led to one of the prison galleries, with two small windows through which the curious would often peer in at us as if we were twin goldfish in a pond. Every sound in the prison entered it, magnified; but it provided the same kind of privacy as a solitary waiting room in a wayside station or a park bench in wintry weather. The room was bare but for two chairs and the desk which divided us; a dim bulb shed a gloomy, unshaded light over our heads as Manuel sat, downcast and miserable, his youthful face an incongruous mask of despair.

What had happened in the three weeks since I had left him, I asked. He gave me, at first, different answers, in different tones of voice, with different degrees of conviction. Shame, panic, hope, and utter confusion jostled together inside him to produce strange patterns of truth and fantasy which were not easy to unravel. He began by putting the blame, squarely, on his family.

"My mother is angry with me," he said. "She told me I shouldn't have asked you for food; she says that was her responsibility. *She* told me I shouldn't see you again."

"What did you say?" I asked him.

"I got mad at her," he said. He repeated this several times. The quarrel sounded genuine enough.

"Then there's my aunt. She's mad at me too. She says I shamed her by asking you to take that message about clothes to the house. I should have asked a girl to do it. She says she's sick of reporters, and that I ought to be content to be forgotten and let her lead her life in peace. So you're not to come and see me any more."

Certainly, something had happened. It looked as if his aunt and mother had objected to Manuel's revealing his need to a stranger. I suspected that his aunt had also been angry that I had seen inside her home. I was not sure about the rest.

There was a pause in the conversation, which unnerved Manuel, and he spoilt his case. "My lawyer too and the prison chaplain—both of them have told me that you should leave me alone."

This was quite unconvincing. I had met his lawyer, who would certainly not have interfered in this way. As for the chaplain, Manuel had always professed indifference, even disdain, toward the cloth.

"And you?" I pressed him. "Would you personally like to carry on?"

"Yes," he said in a small, enormously implausible voice. He sat, guilty, miserable, his eyes downcast, fearing to look up at me. Nothing could have been further from the truth. Whatever his aunt or mother had said to him, the real reasons for his decision lay elsewhere. He was frightened I was going to be angry with him, so I tried again to reassure him. But of course he was not reassured; he was afraid I would talk him into changing his mind. And this he was at all costs determined to prevent.

He started at once on a new tack. "There've been developments in my case, too," he said. "The Supreme Court has thrown out the state lawyer's defense; it had been very badly done. Now one of the private lawyers is working on it instead."

He spoke as if the court were a schoolmaster returning an essay marked "Unsatisfactory—to be done again"; the private lawyer a clever schoolmate willing to help out a backward friend. I expressed surprise.

"Yes," he went on, desperately. "All the minor charges have been dropped and the charge of murder is being reduced to the minimum. And I am to be released tomorrow, or in three weeks' time, on condition that I live a long way out of the city. They are going to sentence me later—next year perhaps—to only a short term of imprisonment." His mother and his lawyer, he said, had made it a condition of their help that he stop seeing me. After release, he would be too far away to be available any more for interview.

I listened to all this in astonishment. He spoke with such conviction that it sounded almost believable; yet it could not possibly be true. I understood then why Celia Rojas had automatically credited his story when ten months before he had casually told her that his parents were millionaires. I might have believed him myself.

At all costs, then, I must be kept at bay. This firm rejection hurt me, deeply, and I showed it. It passed through my mind that I might have said something on some earlier occasion that had wounded him. It was possible, and I decided to ask. To my immense relief, he laughed incredulously. "Lord, no," he said, and smiled, and shook his head.

"But why are you so depressed?" I asked him. He mumbled some excuse.

Then I asked if something had happened in the jail.

"No, nothing," he said, at once. "I've just been bored."

"What's up then?"

"Just depressed, that's all," he said, at last. "I can't sleep, and some days I wake up and want to stay all day in my bunk. I don't want to see anyone—only my family now and then."

We were nearing home now—within hailing distance, in his heart's citadel, of the cell to which he did not have the key. He said no more. I had outstayed my welcome; he was waiting only for me to go.

"Well, Manuel, I hope you won't forget me," I said to him. "I promise I shall not forget you." I was preparing to say goodbye.

Then a strange thing happened. His whole face and voice and body became transformed, shaken by terror and passionate revulsion and distress.

"I can't bear to go on," he pleaded. "I cannot bear to face my thoughts." It had all come back to him; the feelings he never admitted, the guilt he never acknowledged, the horror of striking, bowed beneath him, a defenseless old man in the dark. His act was struggling to become what up till then it had never been: a real part of his life, something for which he was morally responsible. Indeed, it was more than this: he was beginning to see it as a violation, strange and terrible, for which he needed, urgently, forgiveness.

He dared not face this. Terrified, but resolute, he turned back. He saw before him, it seemed to me, a road without destination, a lifetime of boredom streaked with violence, stained by sex. He had tasted its anodynes—the cigarettes, comics, drugs, alcohol, ludo, volleyball—which had always filled the wastes of his vacant hours: the accustomed pleasures of his world.

No matter that he was an outcast in it. On that February afternoon, in that drab office, under those dim rays, he preferred the bleak light of its familiar everyday to the unknown horror of great darkness within him, the newfound land of his heart. Like other voyagers before him, he had not set out, and was not yet prepared, to make his own discovery. In that uncharted country, where every look and every word was as a spear-thrust, he felt encompassed about by his enemies. Of these enemies, I was the most palpable and the most dangerous.

I gave him my address, offered him what personal help and comfort I was able, and said goodbye. I watched him return, briskly, to his cell: he did not look back. So we parted: he to his tribe, I to mine.

VII

This then is the portrait of Manuel Garcés.

He had nothing he could call his own—except his crime. This brought him for a time what all his life he had sought for and never found: attention. No matter that much of it was casual, hostile, and exploitative; it was still attention, precious, beyond his wildest dreams. A stone taken from the seashore, wrapped in brown paper, stained with fish, may not seem much, but it had given him in the eyes of society what his mother's first remembered gift, lost in a children's playground, his brother's borrowed clothes, his social pretences had never done: assured, established status. Manuel Garcés, Teddy boy, murderer: having no personal image to set against it, he accepted this flyblown label like a badge entitling him to membership in a small, distinguished confraternity. The headline cliché opened no doors, provided no magic entrée into criminal society. To his fellows in the prison on the hill he appeared as he had always done: weak, gullible, pretentious, pretty—just one more *gil* ripe for the plucking. In the society of the prison he became again what outside he had, until his crime, always been: no one. He was left again with what in the end he had always been left with: nothing.

VIII

At the end of 1963, some months after I had left for England, when there was still no news of his sentence, I wrote to Manuel for Christmas. He replied, most affectionately; he still hoped to be out of prison in a week or two, and promised to send me his new address. By the beginning of the new year, however, the court had delivered its answer to these hopes: fifteen years. Ten for murder; five for fraud.

Manuel appealed—a standard move in a slow, bureaucratic process, which may well take another two to three years to complete. The different appeal courts will struggle through his dossier, add a year here, dock a year there; the final result will probably not be very different from the first.

Then it will all be over. The name the papers used for their headlines when his crime was fresh will no longer rate a mention in a back page paragraph. Manuel's fate, along with that of thousands of other anonymous men and women, will be lapped in silence and oblivion.

A NOTE ON THE TYPE

THE TEXT of this book is set in *Caledonia,* a Linotype face designed by W. A. DWIGGINS, the man responsible for so much that is good in contemporary book design and typography. Caledonia belongs to the family of printing types called "modern face" by printers—a term used to mark the change in style of type-letters that occurred about 1800. Caledonia borders on the general design of Scotch Modern but is more freely drawn than that letter.

Typography and binding design by
CARL HERTZOG